Simple Facts
About

Self-Publishing

What authors and indie publishers
need to know to produce a great book

Second Edition

Also by Jacquelyn Lynn

Christian Business Almanac: The Ultimate Daily Guide for Kingdom-Driven Entrepreneurs and Leaders

Words to Work By: 31 devotions for the workplace based on the Book of Proverbs

Finding Joy in the Morning: You can make it through the night

Seven Day Anger Free Challenge: Be the Peace

Work as Worship: How Your Labor Becomes Your Legacy (a Conversations book)

How to Survive an Active Shooter: What You do Before, During, and After an Attack Could Save Your Life (a Conversations book)

Faith Words: Color the Words that Inspire You Every Day (a Christian coloring book for adults)

Christian Meditations (a Christian coloring book for adults)

Choices (a Joyful Cup story)

Simple Facts

About

Self-Publishing

What authors and indie publishers
need to know to produce a great book

Second Edition

Jacquelyn Lynn

Simple Facts About Self-Publishing:
What authors and indie publishers need to know to produce a great
book, Second Edition
© 2024 Jacquelyn Lynn

First edition published 2019.

Cover design: Jerry D. Clement
Interior design & production: Tuscawilla Creative Services

Tuscawilla Creative Services
CreateTeachInspire.com

For bulk orders, contact info@contacttcs.com.

This publication is designed to provide accurate and authoritative information in regard to the subject matter covered. It is sold with the understanding that the publisher is not engaged in rendering legal, accounting, or other professional services. If legal advice or other expert assistance is required, the services of a competent professional should be sought.

Library of Congress Control Number: 2024917984

ISBN: 978-1-941826-51-5 (paperback)
        978-1-941826-52-2 (ebook)

For the authors who are brave
enough to put themselves out there
and the readers who make it all
worthwhile

I enjoy self-publishing and sending publishers rejection letters. They're like, 'Who is this guy?' And I'm like, 'the end of your industry.'

~ Ryan Lilly

CONTENTS

1

WHY PUBLISH YOUR BOOK YOURSELF?

S ELF-PUBLISHING ISN'T A NEW idea—it's been around since written language was developed. Some of history's best-known and most prolific writers were self-published: American founding father Benjamin Franklin; English poet, painter, and engraver William Blake; novelist Jane Austen; poet Walt Whitman; *The Shack* author William P. Young; and *Fifty Shades of Grey* author E. L. James, to name a few. And then there's our grandson Jeremiah, who published his own picture books at the age of six and sold them for a dime to his doting grandparents.

You're in excellent company if you self-publish your book.

There's something magical about being a published

author, about having your name on a book, about knowing that people are reading what you wrote. But it's not as easy as it might look. Whatever your goals, if you're going to be successful at self-publishing (or independent publishing, as it's also known), you need to do more than *write* a great book—you need to *publish* a quality book. There's so much more to self-publishing than the manuscript.

Most authors need help getting their books produced and distributed, and there's no shortage of companies serving the self-publishing market. While some are reputable, unfortunately, too many of them charge top dollar for low quality because their customers don't know what to expect and demand. Don't let that frighten you. This book is going to teach you what you need to know about self-publishing so you can either do it yourself or contract with service providers to do it for you without getting ripped off.

Why write a book?

Thanks to technologies such as print-on-demand and digital books, getting a book published is easier than ever, but the first question you need to ask yourself is: *Why* should you write a book?

For business leaders, books are a great marketing tool for you and your company. Saying you are the author of a book in your area of expertise gives you instant credibility. You've established yourself as an expert, and that's an excellent tool for building trust with not only your customers but also with lenders and investors. It also helps establish your company as a leader in your field. A book can be a promotional piece for your business that people will pay to get.

You can use a book to prequalify clients. In the book, you explain what you do, how you do it, and who can use your product or service, then include how to contact you if the reader is interested. Some examples:

- Are you a consultant or professional service provider? Write a book on your area of expertise.

- Does your company sell do-it-yourself supplies for any type of project? Write a book on how to do those projects.

- Do you own a health food store or a gym? Write a book telling people how to get healthy and fit.

You can easily publish this type of book yourself and give a print copy to clients and prospective clients as a gift, as well as make it available for purchase online and in stores. And here's a tip: Take the time to autograph each book you give away personally. That will make it more meaningful to your readers.

Having a print version of your book is not essential to get the benefits of writing a book. Ebooks that address a key issue related to your product or service are a great way to generate sales leads and revenue as well as build your email list. In addition to selling ebooks on all the online bookseller platforms, you can offer them as a free download on your website in exchange for a prospect's name and contact information. We'll talk more about this later when we discuss formatting your books.

What if you're not in business but have a message you want to share? That's another reason to write a book. You don't have to be in business to be an expert on something. Have you had some unique experiences that could be turned into lessons for your readers? Have you researched a particular subject and want to tell others what you've learned? Are you a blogger who wants to turn your blog articles into a book or a pastor who has some great sermons that could become a book? Do you want to write a novel, a children's book, a collection of devotions, or a memoir?

My late aunt did extensive genealogy research on our family. She turned her research into three self-published books. She bought copies for herself and her immediate family then let extended family members know they could find the books on Amazon if they wanted to buy them. She didn't care about making money or selling a lot of copies; she was just looking for an efficient, cost-effective way to share her research with the family.

The list of practical answers to the question of why you should write a book is long, but the most important one is this: Because you want to.

So do it.

Types of publishing

As you consider your self-publishing options, it's important to understand the three basic types of publishers.

1. Traditional. Traditional publishers include the big New York operations and smaller presses around the country. They buy the rights to publish your book and pay you a percentage of the sales (royalties). Traditional publishers make their money on book sales. You don't pay a traditional publisher to publish your book. Depending on the size of the publisher and the sales/revenue potential of your book, you may receive an advance against future royalties. Traditional publishers do all of the production work for you—editing, cover design, interior design, and so on—as well as handling the distribution, all at no cost to you.

2. Self-publishing, also known as independent or indie publishing. This is when you publish your book yourself by handling all of the work or hiring subcontractors, such as editors or cover designers, to help you. Or you may hire a project manager to coordinate everything. The cost to self-publish ranges from minimal (if you do all the work yourself) to hundreds and even thousands of dollars, depending on how much you outsource.

The cost to self-publish ranges from minimal to hundreds and even thousands of dollars, depending on how much you outsource.

3. Hybrid, partner, or pay-to-publish. These are publishers that offer many of the same services that traditional publishers do but charge their authors. The term hybrid comes from combining traditional publishing services with the author-pay model, which used to be known as vanity publishing. While they might earn some money from book sales, the revenue of most hybrid publishers comes from what authors pay for services. Hybrid publishers may also be called self-publishing service companies (SPSC) or partner publishers. The terms under which hybrid publishers operate vary tremendously by company, so if you're considering this route, shop around and do your homework. For an author, this is the most expensive type of publishing. Appendix 2 includes a list of questions to ask a hybrid or partner publisher before signing a contract and paying money.

In Appendix 1, you'll find the text of *Get Your Book Published: How to Choose Between Self-publishing, Traditional Publishing or Pay-to-Publish Options.* This is an ebook I first published as part of my *Conversations* series (a series of narrowly-focused, interview-based books), and it provides more details about the various publishing models, how they have evolved, and how they work. It will help you decide on what will work best for you.

Something most people don't realize is that traditional publishers did a form of pay-to-publish long before today's more transparent model became established. Instead of writing a check to the publisher, authors would guarantee to buy copies (often as many as 10,000-50,000) of their book as part of their publishing agreement. Frequently those publishing contracts would include an advance, but when the authors bought their copies, the publisher made back the advance and more. Whatever the publisher sold over what the author had agreed to buy was a bonus for them. This was a common arrangement with authors who were speakers and could count on substantial back-of-the-room sales at events or with authors who used their books as a marketing tool. Several of my ghostwriting clients over the years negotiated these types of book deals with major publishers. I don't know for sure, but I imagine it's still happening.

Traditional publishers don't guarantee success

Just because a book is traditionally published doesn't mean it will be a bestseller. While you hope the folks at traditional publishers have some superior market insights and skills, they don't always. Stories of celebrity publishing flops are legendary, with well-known people being paid millions of dollars for books that end up selling just a few thousand copies.

Sometimes it's a case of "stuff happens." I ghostwrote a book for a client whose business was in the information products industry (my contract includes a confidentiality clause so I can't reveal the title or publisher). We finished the book on deadline, but the publisher decided to delay publication because it had another book on a similar topic by a better-known author coming out. The idea was not to have the two books competing in the same catalog season. It made sense, but then that better-known author got sued, the seminar business underwent a seismic shift, and my client's promotion plans fell apart. Nobody saw that coming. Sales of his book were decent, but nowhere near as high as they would have been had the book been released earlier.

Traditional publishers can't look into a crystal ball and see the future. They make their forecasts the same way every business does—they research, examine trends, and consider contingencies, then they guess what might happen and hope they're right.

Five publishing industry truths

Before we get into the nuts and bolts of publishing a book, let's take a look at the publishing industry in general. Here are some truths you need to know:

1. There is no magic formula for success. This industry is run by humans, they're all different, and they all make subjective decisions based on their own life experiences. Sometimes they're right, sometimes they're wrong. Most of publishing is a matter of guesswork—and luck plays a big role.

2. Money and profits rule. Publishing is a business. Traditional publishers have to make a profit to stay in business, and most of their profits come from book sales. They have to be confident a book will sell before they accept it for publication. Hybrid or pay-to-publish operations make most (if not all) of their revenue from authors. No matter what they say about your book's potential, if you're paying to get your book published, these publishers don't take any chances—they get paid upfront from the authors. Money and profits are important in indie publishing, too. Your book may be a literary masterpiece but you can't produce it without considering the financial side of the project.

3. The competition is tremendous. No one knows for sure how many books are published each year, but it's a lot. Many industry observers think it's more than one million. Book marketing expert Penny C. Sansevieri says it's more than 4,500 per day. And your competition is not just all those other books—it's movies, television, sports, games, and anything else a potential reader might spend time doing instead of reading your book.

4. Marketing a book takes a lot of work. Even great books by established authors need to be marketed. Whatever publishing route you choose, you're going to have to market your book or it won't sell. A solid book marketing plan begins months before your book is released and continues for months afterward, and the process can cost hundreds and even thousands of dollars.

5. Not everyone will love your book. In fact, some people will hate it, and they'll leave nasty reviews. Your feelings will be hurt. Learn to deal with it.

Pros and cons of pay-to-publish

The hybrid, partner, or pay-to-publish model has benefits and drawbacks you may want to consider. On the benefits side, it's much easier for you as the author because it's a one-stop shop. They'll do everything for you. And in addition to publishing books, some hybrid publishers do a good job of helping authors sell their books.

The two biggest drawbacks are cost and the risk of getting ripped off.

Using a pay-to-publish service is going to cost more than doing it yourself for the same reason that it costs more to hire a plumber to come out and install a new faucet than it does to do it yourself. A hybrid publisher has all the people you're going to need—editors, proofreaders, designers, and so on—so you don't have to find them and vet them. The publisher pays those service providers from the money you pay; they have to mark those fees up so they can make a profit. That's just business.

The other drawback—the risk of getting ripped off—is where you need to exercise caution when considering a pay-to-publish service. There are some ethical firms out there, but a lot of hybrid publishers seem to exist primarily to take advantage of naïve authors.

Here's an example: A ghostwriter friend of mine worked with a client who didn't have much money. He was unemployed and selling his belongings on eBay to pay his rent and buy groceries. But he had an idea for a book that he was sure was going to make him rich.

My friend tried to give her client some realistic advice about what it was going to take to write, edit, produce, and market his book, but that wasn't what he wanted to hear. Somehow he found a pay-to-publish company that played on his dream. He let my friend listen to one of his calls with the salesperson, who did a skilled job of pressuring him to "just get started" with a $3,000 editing package. The salesperson said they would worry about the rest later, even though the client was completely candid about his

There are some ethical firms out there, but a lot of hybrid publishers seem to exist primarily to take advantage of naïve authors.

financial situation. My friend never found out what he ultimately did; she just knew that he dropped her as a ghostwriter. To the best of her knowledge, his book was never published.

Another example: A friend of mine who had never written anything want to write a book. She couldn't decide if she wanted to write an autobiography or a book of devotions. She met someone with a pay-to-publish company who strongly suggested that she sign a contract and pay $3,000 (that must be some sort of a magic number) so that she would be invested in the book and be motivated to actually write it. When she asked what I thought, I told her she had a lot of work to do before she was ready to pay any publishing costs. Fortunately, she followed my advice. It took her more than five years to finish and publish her book; if she had signed that contract, she probably would have lost all or a major part of the $3,000.

The point of sharing these stories is this: If a publisher gives you a high-pressure sales pitch, it should raise a red flag.

Some tips before you decide on a pay-to-publish or hybrid publisher:

Get the full picture before you sign the contract and pay any money. Find out what they're going to do and how much it's going to cost. You want to know every single service they're going to provide and what the ultimate bottom line is going to be. I've heard horror stories of authors who have gotten into pay-to-publish deals at what began as an affordable price but the upselling never ended.

If they promise you the moon, be suspicious. I've said this already, but it's worth repeating: There are no guarantees in publishing. No one can predict how well a book will sell. If a pay-to-publish service promises a huge return on investment through significant book sales, ask for that guarantee in writing—you probably won't get it, but if you do, read it carefully for weasel clauses that will let them avoid responsibility if your book doesn't sell.

Evaluate several different companies. It's the consummate consumer advice: shop around. Don't get so excited about getting your book published that you rush into an agreement without comparing publishers. Do an internet search on the companies you're considering and look beyond the first page of results—go down multiple pages in case they are skilled at hiding negative information. Also, search on the company name plus words like "complaints" or "scams" to see what comes up.

Ask for samples and check references. Are the books they've published well-edited and produced? Actually talk to some of the authors—don't just read testimonials.

Pay with a credit card, PayPal, or other payment app that offers dispute resolution. Even if everything in the proposal looks wonderful, protect yourself by using a payment method that offers you some protection. Never wire money or send checks. This tip applies to how you pay every individual or company you use, whether you're going with a hybrid publisher or taking the do-it-yourself route.

Read and understand the contract. I'll say this over and over: Don't sign a contract unless you understand every word of it. Don't let a salesperson push you to sign a contract that isn't clear or that you're not comfortable with. And remember this: If it's in the contract, it's enforceable; if it's not in the contract, it's not enforceable—no matter what anyone says. Appendix 2 includes questions to ask a pay-to-publish service before you finalize the deal. Be sure the answers to those questions are clearly stated in the contract.

Advantages of self-publishing

Each of the publishing models—traditional, self-publishing (independent), and hybrid—has its advantages and drawbacks. Let's take a look at the specific benefits of publishing your book yourself.

First, you have total control. Even though traditional publishers will consider your input, they have the final say over everything, including the title, the manuscript, the cover and interior design, scheduling, and so on. You'll have input, but they make the final decision. When you self-publish, you have the final say.

Second, you get to keep all the money your book earns. A traditional publisher will usually pay you an advance for your book—typically a few thousand dollars—and then you'll earn royalties based on a percentage of the sale price of the book. Royalty rates are somewhat negotiable, but they're generally in the 12 to 15 percent range. When you function as your own publisher, the difference between the sale price and your cost is yours. So let's say your book sells for $20 and costs $4 a copy to produce. With a traditional publisher, you'll earn about $3 on every sale; if you self-publish, you'll receive $16. Your royalties from a hybrid publisher will vary based on your contract.

Third, you can get a self-published book on the market quickly. The time to market for traditional publishers is usually eighteen months to two years from contract signing. When you self-publish, your book is available as soon as it's written and produced.

Perhaps the biggest advantage of self-publishing is that you can actually get your book published. It's more difficult than ever for an unknown author to get a contract with a traditional publisher, especially for a book that has a narrow market. While self-publishing works for any type of book, it's particularly effective for niche books and books with a concentrated regional appeal. Many authors self-publish with the hope of getting a traditional book deal down the road. That happens. It's not unusual for traditional publishers to approach the indie author of a book that's doing well. Many successful authors use a combination of self-publishing and traditional publishing throughout their careers.

Now that you've got an overview of self-publishing, let's get into the specifics of how to do it.

2

STEPS TO
SELF-PUBLISHING

THE PUBLISHING PROCESS HAS a lot of moving parts—more than you may realize. This chapter will show you the key steps, along with some of the most common mistakes self-publishers make. We'll go into more detail in subsequent chapters.

First, the steps of the process:

1. Write the book. This may seem obvious, but it's often easier said than done. Not everyone who wants to write a book can actually do it. Whether or not you have the necessary writing skills and what to do if you don't is something we'll discuss later, but you can't publish your book until it's written.

2. Have a professional edit the manuscript. Yes, you can—and should—do some self-editing, but that's just the first part of polishing your manuscript. Even the work of the greatest writers can benefit from professional editing.

An editor will make sure your manuscript flows, that it contains all the elements it needs, that the material is logically presented and is appropriate for the intended audience. Editors may suggest additions or deletions, and may work with you through several rounds of editing until your manuscript sparkles.

3. Copyedit and proofread. This step is not the same as editing. A copyeditor checks for clarity and correctness in spelling, punctuation, grammar, math, terminology, and semantics as well as for style consistency. After your manuscript has been designed and formatted, but before it's printed, the proofreader reviews the final proofs, looking for errors and verifying that all the editing and copyediting changes were made.

The steps of the self-publishing process are not necesarily sequential, but they are all essential.

4. Design the cover. Your book's cover is a critical marketing tool and should be professionally designed. It's got to be clear and eye-catching whether it's on a paper version of your book in a store or a thumbnail image on an online bookseller's site.

5. Write the cover copy. Cover copy includes the text on the back cover of print books and sometimes part of the front cover. It's designed to sell the book and should be written by someone who understands how to write marketing copy. It can be paragraphs or a bullet-point list of the advantages of buying and reading the book. Or it can be a list of endorsement quotes from people who have read the manuscript and recommend it.

6. Design the interior. This is what used to be known as typesetting or, more recently, desktop publishing. The interior page design affects your book's readability and reflects on your professionalism.

7. Choose the trim size, binding, cover, and paper. You'll need to choose the physical elements of your book: its page size (trim size), how it's bound, and the weight and color of the paper used for the cover and inside pages.

8. Decide on a publisher. If you are using a pay-to-publish company, it will likely be listed as the publisher. If you are self-publishing, you may think you'll be shown in the book as the publisher. You can be, of course, but your book will look more professional if you create your own publishing entity. We'll discuss how to do that in chapter 7—it's not difficult. This part of the process also includes things like assigning the ISBN, which is an important book identifier we'll discuss in chapter 6.

9. Distribution. Decide how you will get your book into the hands of your readers. Online distribution is easier than ever, but getting your book into bookstores and libraries takes more work. If you're planning to sell books on your own website or at seminars, you'll need a plan for that.

10. Marketing. This is the biggest challenge for all authors, no matter how they're published. What's your plan for getting the word out and making your book stand out so people will want to buy it?

If you're going to be publishing ebooks, these same

steps apply, with the exception, of course, of choosing the physical properties of a print book.

These steps are not necessarily sequential. For example, you may work on the cover design while you're still writing the book. Your distribution and marketing plans should be created early in the process, even though you don't implement them until later on. We'll look at how to incorporate all these steps into your book's business plan in the next chapter.

Common mistakes self-publishers make

There's a big difference between writing a book and publishing one. If you're going the indie publishing route, you need to do both things well.

While there's nothing wrong with—and a lot right with—self-publishing, you don't want your book to look like it's been produced by an amateur. Here are the most common mistakes indie publishers make that you should avoid with your book, whether you're doing it all yourself or hiring people to do it for you:

1. Ineffective title. Instead of coming up with something that *you* think sounds great, come up with a title that will match what your audience is searching for. This is especially important in nonfiction. If you can make it catchy and clever, all the better. But a clever title isn't going to get you any sales if people can't find your book or can't tell what it's about. Your title may include a subtitle, which you can use to clarify the message of your book.

If you're thinking that there have been successful books with titles that didn't seem to have anything to do with the book's content, you're right. But plenty more great books have flopped because of poor titles. Also, most of the time when an author uses a catchy main title, it's with a clarifying subtitle. Take that approach if you want to, but remember there's nothing wrong with a simple, clear title that tells readers what your book is about and helps them decide to buy it.

2. *Poor cover design.* People really do judge a book by its cover, so invest in a professional cover design.

3. *Poor interior design.* The interior design of your book is something most readers won't notice unless it's done wrong. A good interior designer will use professional typefaces, effective spacing, and consistent structure—and pay attention to little things like replacing double hyphens with em dashes and dumb quotes (quotation marks that are straight up-and-down like "this") with smart quotes (quotation marks that curl like "this").

4. *Low-quality graphics.* This applies to both your cover and interior. Image files designed for online use won't look good in print, so be sure your files are the proper resolution. And whether your graphics are photos, charts, diagrams, or whatever, they need to be sharp and professional.

5. *Using copyrighted material without permission.* If you're using material in your book that you didn't create, you need permission from the copyright holder. This applies to both text and images. It's not enough to

simply give attribution; you need permission. There are some exceptions that fall under the fair use provision of the copyright law, but if you're depending on that to protect you against a claim, be sure you understand it and are on solid ground so you don't get sued for copyright infringement.

By the way, using someone else's material without identifying the source and giving proper credit is plagiarism—and it's an even bigger can of worms than copyright infringement. Not only can a charge of plagiarism cost you a lot of money, it can also destroy your reputation, so be sure everything in your book is original or appropriately sourced.

6. Poor editing. The most common reason for negative book reviews (in chapter 11, we'll talk about why you should read negative reviews) and excessive returns is poor editing—or no editing. To repeat: Even the best writers need editors. A professional editor will help you polish your writing until your book shines.

7. Sloppy proofreading. Before you publish your book, after you've made all your final changes, take the time to carefully and thoroughly proofread it—or, better yet, hire someone to do it for you. Check for typos, style consistency, and all those other errors that are so easy to miss while your book is in production but that your readers will spot instantly.

8. Poor book description. Your cover may catch someone's eye, but the book description is what makes them decide to buy. Don't shortchange yourself by writing a brilliant book and a blah description. If you're having trouble with this, consider hiring a marketing copywriter to help you.

9. Trusting friends for feedback. Most of your friends and family members will tell you your book is wonderful, whether it really is or isn't, because they don't want to hurt your feelings. It's okay to get their opinions, and certainly you should ask them for reviews, but get objective feedback for your work in progress from publishing professionals who will be honest with you.

10. Failing to create a plan. You need a business plan for your book. We'll talk more about what to include in your plan in the next chapter.

3

YOUR BOOK'S BUSINESS PLAN

R EGARDLESS OF YOUR SPECIFIC goals for your book, treat your publishing project like it's a small business with a single product. That means starting with a plan.

Model the plan for your book after a traditional business plan because the fundamentals are the same. Just as you would if you were starting a restaurant, a retail store, a professional service practice, or any other type of business, you need a clear picture of your book and the motivation behind it so you can put together the plan to make it happen.

Does the idea of writing a business plan for your book have about as much appeal as a trip to the dentist? For most authors, the answer is yes—and I understand. But let me encourage you to think about it this way: If you're excited about your book, you should be excited about doing the planning that will make it a success.

A good business plan for a book doesn't have to be formal or complicated, but it must be thorough. It will help you refine your idea and get your thoughts organized. Though writing a plan might take more time upfront than you'd prefer to spend, in the long run it will save you time, energy, frustration, and even heartached.

The key is to make it as detailed as necessary to give yourself a roadmap for your project. It also needs to be in writing; it's not enough to have the information in your head.

Creating a business plan for your book forces you to think carefully about what you're doing and why. Like the actual writing of your book, the process of forming a business plan is not necessarily sequential. You'll likely find yourself moving from one section to another and back before you complete it.

What a business plan for a book should include

Let's look at the basic elements of a business plan and how you apply them to a book project. In later chapters, we'll go into more detail about costs, creating a budget, and how to accomplish the elements of your plan, but let's start with the big picture.

Executive Summary

The executive summary is a brief overview of the business, almost a synopsis of the entire business plan. For a book, this is a short description of the book, why you want to write it, and what it will bring to the readers.

Business Description

The business description is a more detailed look at the business. An entrepreneur who is starting a business would begin this section with a look at the entire industry then drill down to the details of the company and what sets it apart from competitors and others in the industry. For your book project, this is where you refine the message of your book; consider any ancillary products such as seminars, speeches, and even promotional items such as t-shirts, mugs and calendars; decide how you're going to publish it; and plan what happens after your book is published.

Market Strategies

The next part of a business plan is defining the market and marketing strategies. An entrepreneur would identify the total market in terms of size, structure, growth prospects, trends, and sales potential, then make a realistic estimate of market share and how it can be reached and captured. For your book plan, this is where you identify who will buy your book—besides your relatives, who probably all think they should get free copies—and how you will market to those buyers.

Remember, no matter how great your book is, your market is not "everyone." You must know who is in your audience if you're going to be able to reach them. And if you have clarified and defined your audience, before you start writing, you'll be more likely to craft a book that will engage them. Your plan should include the specific marketing tactics you'll use along with a budget and schedule.

Competitive Analysis

Next is the competitive analysis. For a business, this is where you identify current and potential competition and analyze their strengths and weaknesses. It's essential to understand the reasons behind their successes and failures so you can fine-tune your own operation. For a book plan, this is where you answer questions such as: What other books are available on your topic? How are they selling? If there are no other books on the topic, is it because no one has thought of it yet or because the idea isn't marketable? If there are a lot of other books on the topic, what will make yours different? Why will people buy it instead of or in addition to similar books? One of the best ways to do this analysis is by searching on Amazon.

Design and Development

The next element of a business plan is a section on design and development. For a product, you would describe the design and outline its development within the context of production and marketing. For a book, figure out how you're going to turn your idea into a manuscript. Do you have the time and skill to write it yourself? Do you need to hire researchers? Do you need a ghostwriter? What about editing services? And how long is it going to take to get everything done?

Operations and Management

For a business, this section demonstrates how the

company will function on a continuing basis, who is responsible for what aspects of the operation, how those functions will be carried out, and the capital and expense requirements. For a book, this is where you decide on which type of publishing you're going to do and who is going to do the work.

If you want to go with a traditional publisher, you'll need to create a book proposal and find a literary agent. That process is beyond the scope of this book, but there are plenty of other books and resources out there that will tell you how to do that. If you want to use a pay-to-publish company, you need to figure out exactly what services it will provide and what it will cost. If you're going to self-publish and outsource some of the work such as editing, proofreading, and design, how will you find these sources? How will you evaluate them? How much are you willing to pay them? How will you manage them so your book stays on schedule?

Financial Components

The last section of a business plan includes the financial components. This is the real backbone of a plan and should include an income statement, cash flow statement, and balance sheet. Pull these numbers from the other areas of your plan. How much will you spend on getting the book written? Include the cost of research, a ghostwriter if you hire one, editing, design, and so on. What are your production costs (cover and interior design, printing, graphics, and so on)? What will it cost to implement your marketing plan? Now, look at what you can realistically expect the book to earn, whether that's in actual sales of the book or ancillary sales, and how long it will take for you to receive the revenue.

Evaluate your plan

Will your plan work? Of course, you won't know for sure until you implement it. But there are some reasons why a plan for a business and a plan for a book might fail. As you evaluate your plan, make sure it doesn't include any of these shortcomings:

The plan is incomplete. Leaving out any of the elements sets you up for failure.

The plan makes unfounded or unrealistic assumptions. Of course, you'll have to make some assumptions and maybe even some guesses, but most of your plan should be based on facts.

The plan says you have no competition. Even if your book is unique, it will have competition.

The plan doesn't plan. Your business plan should be a roadmap that will take you through the process of writing, publishing, marketing, and selling your book.

When you've got your plan together, you'll be ready to write and publish a book that will help you achieve your goals.

4

WRITING, EDITING, AND PROOFREADING YOUR BOOK

Now that you've got your plan, it's time to write.

Though this isn't a book on how to write, I'll briefly share how I do it. My approach is fairly structured. For non-fiction (whether I'm writing my own material or ghostwriting for a client), I think about everything the book needs to include and write it all down in several brainstorming sessions. I keep a doc file on my phone so I can add ideas that come to me when I'm not actively brainstorming. I don't worry about the order or the details; I just list all the key points. When that's done, I go back and organize everything I listed into chapters that have a logical flow. Then I write based on that outline. I take a similar approach to fiction by coming up with the main story concept, listing the scenes so I know what has to happen to move the plot along, organizing them into a logical sequence, then doing the actual writing. Other writers just sit down and write, letting the work lead them.

In the publishing world, these two styles are known as plotters and pantsers. I'm a plotter—I plan everything out before I start writing. Pantsers are called that because they fly by the seat of their pants and let the work lead them. And some writers combine the two approaches. One is not right, the other is not wrong. Do whatever suits you best.

What if you're not a writer? It's possible that even though you have a great message, you may not have the writing skill necessary to craft a readable manuscript. If you don't love writing and/or you're not good at it but you still want to publish a book, consider hiring a ghostwriter—a professional writer who can take your ideas and wordsmith them into a book. A variation on ghostwriting is to hire a collaborator who will work with you and may or may not get bylined credit (either as an equal, as in "John Smith *and* Mary Jones" or in a support role, as in "John Smith *with* Mary Jones" or "John Smith *as told to* Mary Jones").

Hiring and working with a ghostwriter

A ghostwriter is paid to write books, articles, blogs, or other content that is officially credited to another person. While it's common for celebrities, executives, politicians, and even some bestselling fiction authors to hire ghostwriters to produce their written materials, you don't have to be in one of those categories to benefit from the services of a talented ghostwriter.

Ghostwriting arrangements can vary significantly from one where the named author (the person whose byline is on the book) simply establishes the concept and the ghostwriter completely researches and produces a final manuscript to one where the named author writes most of the first draft and the ghostwriter or collaborator cleans it up—and anything in between.

Due to the nature of the business (ghostwriters often work under stringent confidentiality clauses), it's impossible to know how many books were written all or in part by ghostwriters, but some industry observers suggest that named authors and publishers spend as much as $500 million or more every year on the services of ghostwriters. Why? Because it's a worthwhile investment. Good ghostwriters can save you a tremendous amount of time, help you turn your information into a marketable book, and enhance your reputation by the quality of their work.

Ghostwriters and collaborators are professionals and should be treated and compensated as such. For example, don't ask them to write your book for nothing now and the promise of payment when (if) the book sells. Would you work under those terms? You can certainly incorporate a percentage of revenue from sales of your product into your agreement as a bonus, but don't suggest making it the only source of compensation for the writer. Remember, this project may be your passion—but to a ghostwriter or collaborator, it's a job.

What should you look for in a ghostwriter (who writes the book *for* you) or collaborator (who writes the book *with* you)? The necessary skills for either function are similar; I'm going to talk more about ghostwriters because it's a more common term. Also, many people who call themselves ghostwriters are open to collaborating on projects.

First and most important, you want someone with excellent writing skills. There are plenty of people out there who call themselves ghostwriters who can't write, so ask to see writing samples from the writers who are candidates for your project. As I've said, many ghostwriters are bound by confidentiality clauses and may not be able to show you everything they've written, but they should be able to show you enough for you to determine how well they write.

As you review the samples, consider the writer's style. Ideally, you want a ghostwriter who can write in your voice—meaning that what they write sounds like you. It's easier to achieve this if your respective natural styles are similar.

In addition to style, consider the writer's knowledge of the subject. Good ghostwriters can quickly learn about any subject from the named author and other research sources, but it's helpful—though not essential—if they start with some familiarity and interest in the topic.

You should also consider the writer's overall experience. Certainly everybody is a beginner at some point, and that someone is a beginner is not by itself a valid reason for not using them, but as writers gain experience, they also gain market knowledge and connections that may be of benefit to you. Of course, experience usually comes with a price—you'll likely pay higher rates to a more experienced writer.

Finally, consider your compatibility with the writer. Ghostwriters and their clients usually spend a lot of time together and get to know each other very well. Depending on the subject matter of your book, you may need to reveal a lot of personal information to get it written, so choose a ghostwriter with whom you'll be comfortable doing this.

Once you've selected a writer and agreed on the scope of the project and the fee, put it all down in a detailed contract. This clarifies your agreement and prevents any potential misunderstandings. The contract should:

- Stipulate the relationship (typically, the ghostwriter is an independent contractor, not an employee);
- Provide details on the payment amounts and schedule;
- Include a description of the work plan and schedule, as well as how revisions will be handled;

- Outline who is responsible for what when it comes to research;

- Clearly define the ownership of research materials, other intellectual property, the work in progress, and the finished work;

- Include an appropriate confidentiality agreement; and

- Address standard contractual issues such as termination (how and when the contract can be canceled), legal written notice (how notice of project-related issues should be provided), severability (a provision that if one part of the contract is deemed to be unenforceable for any reason, the remainder of the contract still applies), arbitration (a way of settling a dispute outside of going to court), indemnification (a "hold harmless" provision that specifies how the parties will be compensated for losses or damages that arise from the project), and venue (the place where a lawsuit should be filed).

What do editors do?

In the publishing industry, a lot of people with vastly different job descriptions hold the title of editor. Before you hire an editor, be clear on what services you'll get. These are the primary types of editing your manuscript may need:

Developmental editing. Also called content or

substantive editing, this is when an editor gives you big-picture feedback and direction. If your idea is still in a rough stage, a strong developmental editor with vision can save you a lot of time by helping you bring structure and organization to your book. If you've already written your book, you may be dismayed when a developmental editor sends you back to your computer to rewrite it. Don't take it personally and do seriously consider every one of their suggestions.

Copy editing. When you think your book is complete, it's time to send it to a copy editor. This editor looks at the details, reviewing your book for overall readability; perhaps rewriting sentences or even paragraphs for clarity; correcting spelling, grammar, and punctuation; correcting typos; checking for style consistency; and generally making sure there are no mistakes in your manuscript.

Before you hire an editor, be clear on what services you'll get.

Proofreading. The last step in the editing process is proofreading. The proofreader makes sure no spelling or grammar errors make it into the final version of your manuscript. Your book should undergo a second round of proofreading after the manuscript has been produced—that is, after the text has been placed into the interior design of your book. This is your chance to check for any confusing or clumsy page and word breaks that may have happened with the file conversion, and review issues like checking page numbers in the table of contents, captions on illustrations, and the headers and footers on the pages. Finally, you should proofread the paper proof of your book before it is released. Technology is wonderful, but gremlins can find their way into digital files, so give your book one final careful check before you publish it.

Beta and sensitivity readers

A beta reader is not an editor but what they do falls loosely under the editing category. Beta readers are usually unpaid test readers (although you can find people who will beta read for a fee) who will give you feedback from the perspective of an average reader. Beta readers can be your close friends, but it's better if they're not because you're likely to get more honest feedback from people who aren't worried about

> *When you get feedback from beta readers, take the time to digest it and then decide if you want to incorporate or ignore their suggestions.*

damaging your relationship with criticism. How many beta readers you have is a judgment call. Most authors find that five or six can give them the input they need; some prefer to use more.

Beta readers are not editors or proofreaders, and you shouldn't expect them to get down in the weeds of manuscript construction. What you want them to do is react to your book as your audience will. You want beta readers who love to read, are familiar with your genre, and will be honest with you. Because they know the genre, they'll be able to evaluate how well your manuscript compares to other books.

It's helpful if you give your beta readers some guidelines so they know what type of feedback you're seeking. Provide a list of questions for them to answer. You should also give your beta readers a clear deadline. Depending on the length of your book, it's realistic to let them take a month or so to read it and get back with you.

Different authors use beta readers at different stages of their projects. I recommend getting your book as close to final as possible then share it with your beta readers. When you get their feedback, don't implement it right away. Take the time to digest it and then decide if you want to incorporate or ignore their suggestions. Make whatever changes you agree with, then send your manuscript out for professional editing. When your book is published, show your appreciation to your beta readers by sending them a signed copy. If you include an acknowledgments section, you may want to list them there.

If you're writing fiction with characters whose backgrounds are different from yours, or if you're writing nonfiction but need to address issues related to diversity, you may want to have a sensitivity reader review your manuscript to make sure what you wrote doesn't inadvertently offend or anger your ultimate readers. Sensitivity readers can help you avoid stereotypes, create realistic characters, and write a better book. Though beta readers are typically not paid, sensitivity readers are.

You can learn more about beta readers and sensitivity readers by doing an internet search on the terms.

Before you send your manuscript to anyone

Before you send your manuscript to anyone—an editor, proofreader, beta reader, or anyone else you want input from—make sure it is as close to perfect as you can make it for its stage of development. Self-edit ruthlessly. You know what you meant to say; be sure that's what you actually said. Read it out loud to see how it flows. Check for typos and spelling errors by reading your manuscript backward. Use editing tools like Grammarly and ProWritingAid that will check punctuation, sentence construction, overused words and phrases, and more.

You may want to follow my personal policy, which is never to let anyone see anything I've written that isn't my best. Once, when I was speaking about freelancing for magazines to a class at the College of Journalism and Communications at the University of Florida, a student asked if it was okay to send his first draft to an editor. My response was, "Only if you never want to get an assignment from that magazine again." Even though you're self-publishing and don't have to worry about assignments from publications, never let sub-quality work get out of your hands.

Once your manuscript is complete—written, edited, polished, and proofed—it's time to turn it into a book.

5

PRODUCING YOUR BOOK

PRODUCING YOUR BOOK IS the process of taking your completed manuscript and turning it into a published book. That includes cover and interior design as well as creating and formatting what's known as front and back matter.

The design of your book showcases your content. If you've ever bought or sold a house, you've probably heard the term *curb appeal*, meaning what the house looks like from the curb. A house with a freshly-cut lawn, healthy shrubs, and new paint has greater curb appeal and will attract more prospective buyers than one with more weeds than grass, dead plants, and peeling paint. That's not to say that the shabby-looking house isn't great on the inside—it might be, but a lot of prospective buyers won't bother to get that far.

The same principle applies to books. Of course,

the key part of a book's "curb appeal" is the cover, but readers will also consider the interior design—or format—before they look at the actual content. Small text, narrow margins, line spacing that is too narrow or too wide, fonts that are inappropriate or hard to read, and other design mistakes all send the message that this book is going to be difficult on the eyes and the content may not be worth the effort it will take to read it.

Whether you're going to do the design yourself, use a template, or hire someone to do it for you, your first step is to understand the elements of a well-designed book and cover. After you read this chapter, go to a bookstore and browse through all the best-sellers in your genre. Study the cover and interior design. Look at the typeface (fonts), margins,

Your first step is to understand the elements of a well-designed book and cover.

leading (the space between the lines of type), the placement of the front and back matter (which we'll discuss in this chapter), the use and placement of images, and so on. Make notes on what you like and don't like so you can model your book after what looks good and is attractive to readers.

Ebooks and print books should be formatted differently. While several online publishing platforms offer to convert your ebook to a print book or your print book to an ebook, I recommend handling that yourself. They might do an acceptable job converting your print file to an ebook file, but it's unlikely an automated system will be able to convert an ebook file to a professional-looking print book. I believe you'll get a better product if you format each version yourself from the start. We'll talk more about that later in this chapter. Let's begin with choosing your production tools.

What apps should you use?

Publishers have a wide range of choices when it comes to production applications. For your book's interior, some (InDesign, QuarkXPress) are complex and have steep learning curves; others, like Microsoft Word, are easier to use. If you understand the fundamentals of good design, you can create an attractive book using Word or the free Apache OpenOffice or LibreOffice. For the cover, again you have a choice between complex (Photoshop, Illustrator) and various low-cost or free cover design products that are easier to use (Canva is a popular one; you can also do an internet search on "free book cover design tools"). And, of course, you can always outsource these functions to freelance professionals.

Cover design

It's a cliché but it's true: People judge a book (and its author) by its cover. Your book's cover gives prospective readers a sense of what the book is about. The cover should convey a mood, even tell a story. It needs to invite the reader to pick it up in a bookstore or click on the image online. And it needs to reflect favorably on you.

The first step of the cover design process is to think

about the message your cover needs to convey. Figure that out, focus on it, and keep it in mind until you have your cover finalized. Reject anything that moves you away from that key message, no matter how creative or cool it might be. If your book is going to be part of a series, keep that in mind as you design the first cover so you can make the covers for subsequent books identifiable as part of the series.

Publishing consultants routinely advise their clients to hire a professional book cover designer, and I agree. But not every person who claims to be a professional cover designer does quality work. They will not always capture the essence of your book.

Know what's appropriate and popular for covers in your genre.

It's important that you study cover design trends and control the process as much as you can. Keep in mind that the cover designer is not going to read your book. They're going to design the cover based on what you tell them, and they may not always get it right the first time. If they miss the mark, ask them to make changes.

I've had to do this many times over the years. working with traditional publishers and as a self-publisher. If the cover isn't right, explain what needs to be changed and let the designer try again.

Even though you'll hire a cover designer, you should know what's appropriate and popular in your genre. For example, romance readers like pictures of the main character(s) on the cover. If you write fiction and include a photo that's supposed to represent your character on the cover, be sure the model really does look like your character. Readers get irritated when the woman on the cover has dark hair and the character in the book is a blonde. While it might seem silly, they'll leave negative reviews over it.

I'm not a big fan of using stock photography on book covers. I know it's common and, in many cases (like romance and some other popular fiction genres), essentially required. Though I've seen stock photos beautifully blended into a cover, if you don't purchase exclusive rights to the image, there's always the chance that the image you use will also be on a competitive book—or worse, a book with a conflicting message. If you're interested in using stock photography, do a search on "buy stock photos" for more information and a list of stock photo agencies. You can license the use of a photo for a modest fee (it varies with the source, but often can be just a few dollars), but that means others may also use the image. Or you may be able to buy exclusive rights to the photo for a substantial sum (several hundred dollars or more) and know that no one else can use it.

Be cautious when using "free" or "public domain" images and never use an image you find on Google without permission.

Whether you purchase the image yourself or a cover designer buys it, use a reputable agency and be clear on the rights you are acquiring. Be cautious when using "free" or "public domain" images and never use an image you find on Google without permission. If you do, you may find out the hard way that you've used an image that belongs to someone who could sue you for damages and make you remove the image from your cover.

Choose a typeface for your title, subtitle, byline, and other cover text that matches the message of your book and the mood of your images, and is easy to read. Your cover text is as much of a design element as anything else, so make it work for you. And don't put "by" before your name on the cover—professionally designed covers simply include the author's name.

Invest time in studying the covers of popular, similar, and competing books so you can judge your cover and reduce the risk of a design mistake. When you find covers that you either love or hate, share them with your designer. Provide specific notes about the elements, such as "I love the image" or "the colors are striking but I don't like the title font."

If you're only going to publish your book in digital format, you'll only need a front cover. If you're going to have a print version, you'll need a front and back cover plus a spine. The back cover will include promotional copy describing your book and/or endorsements from readers (I'll explain how to get those endorsements in chapter 10). Because any promotional copy should describe the book in a way that will make someone want to buy it, it's a good idea to have someone skilled in creating marketing copy write this for you. The back cover should also include the publisher, category, price, ISBN, and barcode, and may include a brief author bio and photo.

The spine should include the book's title, the author's name (either last name only or first and last name, depending on the size of the spine), and the publisher's imprint. If you're self-publishing, come up with an imprint to use for your publishing operation. We'll talk about how to do that in chapter 7. If your goal is to have your book in retail stores or libraries, it must have the title on the spine—stores and libraries won't stock books that don't. And even if you don't care about having your book on retail shelves, consider that having the title on the spine makes it easier for readers to locate the book on their own bookshelves.

Remember that bookstore buyers, librarians, and other wholesale book buyers who purchase books for resale have a sharp eye for distinguishing professional versus amateur book covers. Be sure your cover will stand up to their scrutiny.

If you've got some good cover concepts and you're not sure which is best, get input from your prospective readers. One way to do that—and it will also generate some pre-publication buzz for your book—is to create a social media poll and ask your followers to vote for the cover they like best.

How do you find book cover designers? One way is to check books with covers that you like—the cover designer will often be credited either on the copyright page or in the acknowledgments. You may be able to find that without seeing the physical book by using Amazon's "look inside" feature. You should also read what Marla Markman says about finding and working with cover designers in *Get Your Book Published* in Appendix 1.

Inside your book

There's a lot more to the interior of your book than just your manuscript. Let's look at the elements you need to include:

Front and back matter

As the name suggests, the front and back matter includes the material that is not part of your manuscript but that needs to be in your book. Some of the front and back matter elements specifically belong at the front or back of your book; others can go either place. The elements you'll typically have to deal with in your book include:

- *Half title.* A page that contains only the title of the book and is usually the first page you see when you open the book or the first page after your endorsement quotes. Many authors use this page when they autograph books because it has plenty of space on which to write. It should be on the right-hand page when the book is open.

- *Title page.* Includes the title, subtitle, author, and publisher. You may also include the publisher's location, year of publication, and some brief information about the book. Some publishers use a black-and-white version of the cover for the title page. The title page typically follows the half title page on the next right-hand page.

▤ *Copyright page.* Includes the copyright notice, edition information, publication details, printing history, cataloging data, any legal notices or disclaimers, and the ISBNs. It's common for credits for design, production, editing, and illustration to be on the copyright page. Copyright permissions (if you have used copyrighted information in the book) may also be on the copyright page. The copyright page goes in the front of a printed book, usually on the back side of the title page, but may be moved to the back in an ebook version.

▤ *Dedication and/or epigraph (an inspirational quote).* Not every book includes these elements, but when they do, they follow the copyright page on the right-hand page. Some authors use epigraphs at the beginning of each chapter.

▤ *Table of contents (or contents).* Lists the book's chapters, sections, and other major divisions. Typically the table of contents in a print book will include the page numbers of the items; in an ebook, the contents list consists of links to that material in the book.

📚 *List of figures and tables.* For books containing numerous figures and/or tables, a list of these items in the front of the book is helpful to readers.

📚 *Foreword.* A short piece written by someone other than the author designed to give context and credibility to the book. Forewords are not essential, but if your book has one, include the name of the writer and any important identification and/or credentials.

📚 *Preface.* Written by the author, explaining how the book came into being. As with forewords, prefaces are not required and are often skipped over by readers.

📚 *Acknowledgments.* Where the author lists and thanks the people who have contributed to the book. Historically, acknowledgments have been placed in the front matter, but increasingly in contemporary books they are going in the back of the book.

📚 *Promotional blurbs.* These brief endorsement quotes about this book and other works by the author are usually placed at the very front of a print book so they're one of the first things a prospective book buyer sees.

- *Other works by the author.* A list of books and other major works by the author that can be a part of either the front or the back matter.

- *Author bio.* A brief biography and photo of the author. This may include contact information, a website, social media links, or an offer to encourage the reader to connect with the author. The author bio is part of the back matter.

- *Appendix.* Appendices are supplements to the main work placed at the end of the book.

- *Glossary.* An alphabetical list of terms used in the book and their definitions. Glossaries are typically part of the back matter, although you may include some definitions within the main text of your manuscript.

- *Bibliography.* A list of books and other sources referred to in the book. Generally, only scholarly books include bibliographies and they are part of the back matter.

- *Index.* An alphabetical list of names, places, subjects, events, etc., with the page numbers indicating where they are mentioned in the book. Typically, only technical or historical non-fiction books that are likely to be used as reference sources include indexes, and they are part of the back matter.

- *Pages with ads promoting other books,*

products, or services. These pages are part of the back matter. Some publishers use them to promote works by other authors. You may use them to promote yourself, your company, and various products you are selling.

The middle: your book

Between the front and back matter is your book—that manuscript you've likely labored over for so long. As I've said, this isn't a book on how to write, but as you write, you may want to consider what your book will look like. For example, avoid paragraphs that are so long the reader may get lost. Use subheads and lists in non-fiction books to help break up the page and guide the reader. Pictures, charts, graphs, sidebars, and

Will your design elements work as you intend?

Getting creative with your design elements can result in a striking, attractive book—or they can be a total flop.

I read a book that was beautiful but the designer emphasized key points with underlines that looked like smudged pencil marks. Several reviewers commented that they'd received used books that had already been marked up. When I saw the first mark, I wondered the same thing, but then realized it was part of the design.

Innovative design is great as long as it supports rather than detracts from your content.

callouts are all elements that could go into your book. We'll discuss the design aspect of how to include them in the next section.

Interior design for print books

Designing the interior of a book is one of those much-harder-than-it-looks things. A poorly-designed book will halt readers before they get past the first page. The best content in the world will have a hard time overcoming an amateurish or ineffective design.

Years ago, a major publisher of business books decided to venture into the pay-to-publish arena. I happened to be the ghostwriter for the first author they published under these terms. Fortunately for my client, I understood what the interior of the book should look like. The first version the publisher's designer produced was terrible—the spacing between the lines was too tight, the chapter title and subhead font was childish rather than professional, the pages were littered with cheesy icons, and there were other issues I don't recall now. I insisted on changes. The designer argued with me, telling me that this was a design the executive editor liked. I told him I didn't care what the executive editor liked, my client was paying the bill and the design wasn't acceptable.

He made some changes that were better but not good enough, so I rejected that version. I think he ended up doing five or six rounds of design revisions before I was satisfied (he could have only done one if he'd followed the instructions I gave him the first time, but he chose not to). In our last conversation, after I finally decided the book was acceptable, the designer told me I was the most difficult client he'd ever worked with. Given his initial design and what the book finally looked like, I took that as a compliment. And he should have thanked me for pushing him to create a book that looked good.

Here are some of the issues you need to understand about book design:

Trim size. This is the height and width of the pages of your book, and it's the first design decision you need to make. It affects both your cover and interior design. Use a standard trim size; non-standard sizes increase your design, production, printing costs.

Color or black & white. Your cover, of course, will be full color. Even if you choose a black-and-white or grayscale cover design, the print process will technically be color. All printers are set up for that. But will your interior be color or black-and-white? It depends on your content (see the next paragraph about photos and graphics) and goals for your book. Color increases production costs, although technology is making full-color interiors more affordable.

Photos and other graphics. Will your book include pictures, drawings, charts, illustrations, and other graphics? If so, will they be placed throughout the text or in a section of their own? Similar elements include callouts (a short string of text set aside from the main text with graphic elements, also referred to as *extracts*) and sidebars (a section of text typically the length of a short article set aside from the main text). Remember that various design elements can add style (good) or clutter (distracting) to your pages. Use them cautiously.

Typography. The art and technique of arranging type is known as typography. It involves selecting typefaces, point sizes, line lengths, line spacing, and letter spacing. Prior to the development of digital design and printing, there was a clear difference between the terms typeface (the design of type, such as Arial or Times New Roman) and font (size, weight, and style). Nowadays, the terms are used interchangeably. The typography of the interior of your book has a significant impact on its readability and eye-appeal.

Page margins. Don't be tempted to use narrow margins to get more words on the page; it will only reduce your book's readability. Look at books from established publishers and see what size margins they use. You need to consider both visual appeal and whether you want your readers to be able to make notes in the margins. Another important point: the inside margin (the one closest to the spine) should be wider than the outside margin to accommodate the spine so the margins look equal when the book is printed. You don't want your text slipping into the binding area. At a casual glance, all four margins should appear close in size.

Running heads and page numbers. Generally, the top margin of each page will include a running head with the book's title on one side and the author's name or current chapter title on the other. The page number (called *folio* in book production) can be included in either the top or bottom margin. Odd-numbered pages should be on the right—always, no exceptions. Do not include the running head or page numbers on your front and back matter pages or on any pages intentionally left blank.

Leading (the spacing between the lines). Don't use the default single or double spacing of whatever design program you're using. You may need to experiment with the leading until you find the spacing that works best for your typeface. If there's not enough space between the lines, the material is harder to read and can cause eye strain. Too much space is also distracting. A good guideline is to set the leading at least two points greater than the type size.

With both page margins and leading, you need to

Standard book sizes

The standard book sizes in the various genres are:

Fiction: 4.25"x6.87", 5"x8", 5.25"x8", 5.5"x8.5", 6"x9"

Novella: 5"x8"

Children's: 7.5"x7.5", 7"x10", 10"x 8"

Textbooks: 6"x9", 7"x10", 8.5"x11"

Non-fiction: 5.5"x8.5", 6"x9", 7"x10"

Memoir: 5.25"x8", 5.5"x8.5"

Photography: Whatever size works for your project

consider what's called "negative space" or "white space." Those design terms refer to any space with nothing on it, and it's a critical element in design. If everything on the page is screaming for your readers' attention, nothing will stand out. Negative space is one of the easiest ways to help your reader see what's there without distraction, and it adds style and elegance to the page.

Subheads. Fiction books usually don't have subheads, although it's possible your story could lend itself to that type of design. Non-fiction books have anywhere from one to four levels of subheads. The subheads should be a little larger than the main text. Develop a consistent hierarchy of subhead levels identified by type size and face, indentation, color (use shades of gray in a black and white book), and other design elements. Get ideas from published books that have an eye-appealing design.

Design of each chapter's first page. Consider the style of the first page of each chapter. Typically the actual text of the chapter will start about a third of the way down the page, with the chapter number and title at the top. Don't include a running head on the first page of a chapter.

You may want to include a graphic element at the beginning of each chapter, but it isn't necessary. In my novel *Choices*, I use a coffee cup with the chapter number on the side of the cup because so much of the story takes place in a coffee shop. In my other books, I use a consistent style for the chapter number and title, usually without a graphic element.

Professional designers typically do not indent the first paragraph of each chapter or the first paragraph of sections in the chapter. On the first page, use a drop cap (the first letter is larger than the rest of the text and takes up two or three lines) at the beginning of your first paragraph.

The standard for non-fiction books is for each chapter to start on an odd-numbered or right-hand page, even though it may mean leaving some left-hand pages blank. For fiction books, that's a design call you'll make based on what you like and what works for your book. It's easier for readers to find chapters if they all begin on a right-hand page.

If you're going to do your own interior design, take the time to study current trends and best practices. Start with an internet search on phrases like "how to design a book interior" and "interior book design" to find articles and tips that will help you.

Part opener page. If your book has parts, decide on a consistent design for the part opener page, which is the page that introduces the part. It should begin on the right-hand page and include a part number and optional title. One way to distinguish the part opener page from the chapter first page is to use Roman numerals for or spell out the part number and Arabic numerals for (or spell out if you used Roman numerals) the chapter numbers. For example: Part I and Chapter One, or Part Two and Chapter 2. Some designers don't use the word "part," especially if there is a title.

The part opener page may include an introduction to the part. If you have text other than the part number and title, you should number the page; if you don't, the page should not be visibly numbered.

The trim size of your book

The term trim size refers to the final size of a book's page. Commercial printers often print multiple pages on a large single sheet of paper and trim it down to the finished size—the trim size. What's the best trim size for your book? It depends.

For many years, a popular trim size for non-fiction books was 6"x9". Apparently, at some point, some

Do it yourself with templates

If you're not a trained designer but you still want to do your own interior production, consider finding a good template. I like and have used the templates from Book Design Templates. They have a wide range of choices with recommendations for how to use them (fiction, non-fiction, children's, picture books, etc.) and they're available in formats for multiple popular design applications (as of this writing, Word, Pages, and InDesign).

Book Design Templates also offers a cover design service and other products designed to help self-published authors market their books.

Visit CreateTeachInspire.com/resources for links to learn more about Book Design Templates.

pundits said it was best and the industry followed along. However, with the proliferation of self-published authors who chose this trim size, traditional publishers began choosing other trim sizes to differentiate their books. The casual reader isn't likely to notice this, but reviewers and bookstore buyers might, so keep that in mind when you choose your trim size.

Issues to consider when deciding on trim size include:

The standard for your genre. Check out the trim sizes of recent (within the past two years) bestsellers in your genre. Workbooks, for example, will have larger pages than text-only books. A simple how-to manual might have a smaller trim size, but a how-to manual with lots of diagrams and pictures may need larger pages.

The standard sizes your printer offers. Standard sizes generally cost less to print and can be printed faster because the printer is already set up to do them.

The length of your book. This is not an absolute rule, but often shorter books have a smaller trim size to increase the page count.

Your audience. What will your readers prefer? Who is going to be buying and reading your book, and what will they find most comfortable?

Choosing the best fonts

The most important rule for choosing your book's fonts is this: Do *not* use the default fonts of whatever program you're using to set your book up. If you do, your book will look boring and amateurish.

A good rule to follow is to choose two fonts for the interior of your book—one for chapter titles and section heads and one for the body copy. These two fonts need to look different but be compatible.

If you're not a professional designer, you probably can't look at a font and know what it is—in fact, many professional designers can't do that, either. But they know what works well together.

Some tips for how to approach choosing fonts if you're using a professional designer: Let them know the mood and tone you want to create and trust their judgment, or find a published book you like and send them some sample pages to use as a model.

If you're doing your own design, do an internet search on phrases like "best font pairs for books" or "popular typefaces for books" to find fonts that work for you.

Do you need a large print version of your book?

For people who are visually impaired but still prefer to read rather than listen to audiobooks, large print books are a great option. You may want to consider a large print version of your book if your audience includes:

- Low-vision readers
- Middle-aged and senior readers who are developing presbyopia
- Students of all ages who spend a lot of time

reading

- People who spend a lot of time in front of computers

- People with physical dexterity problems, learning disabilities, brain injuries, or cognitive impairment

More than two billion people around the world have some type of vision impairment, which means the audience for large print books is significant. Top selling large print categories include fiction, religion, business, health, and self-help.

Large print is not just a publishing term for using a bigger font size. A large print book is going to be designed differently than your regular print edition.

To set up a large print book, you should:

- Use a font size of at least 14 points and no larger than 20 for the body text (16-18 is ideal in most cases; a common guideline is twice the minimum acuity size); titles and headings should be larger

- Choose an easy-to-read, sans serif font designed for legibility that makes it easy to distinguish one character from another

- Do not use any italics, bold, underlining, superscripts, or big blocks of capitalization

- Do not include any information that is conveyed solely through images or diagrams

- Create a clear, consistent layout with

adequate line spacing and left-aligned text

▤ Avoid hyphenation between lines

▤ Provide adequate contrast between the paper and text (black and white is classic and always safe)

▤ Use non-glossy paper

▤ Add a large print badge to the spine or cover

With print-on-demand publishing, your primary cost in creating a large print edition is the interior design work. However, creating a large print book will add to your page count, which makes your large print edition more expensive to print. You may want to consider using a larger trim size than your regular print edition to keep the page count lower.

Having a large print edition is an important service to your readers and could significantly increase your sales.

Interior design for ebooks

In the vast majority of cases, if you have a print book, you're going to want an ebook version. And sometimes you'll skip the print version and only publish ebooks.

The most important thing to remember about designing the electronic version of a print book is that your design must accommodate a variety of e-readers. Ebooks may be read on dedicated e-readers (such as Kindles and Nooks), tablets, phones, or computers, which means you don't want a fixed layout. Your ebook file should have reflowable text so that if the reader adjusts the fonts, the book will automatically reorganize itself.

Just as I recommended studying bestselling print books for design ideas, do the same with ebooks. Read other books to see what works and what doesn't.

Many print-on-demand services provide print-to-ebook and ebook-to-print conversion services. Never use the automatic ebook-to-print conversion; you should always design your print book from the start. You can try the print-to-ebook conversion tool and see if you

When a fixed layout ebook works

There may be times when you want to provide an ebook in a fixed layout with images and various design elements. In those cases, create the file as a pdf to preserve your design.

One of the most common reasons to produce an ebook in a fixed layout is when you're using the book as a lead generator. For example, you might offer the ebook as a free download from your website in exchange for someone signing up for your mailing list.

While those ebooks can be full-length books with print versions, more often they are much shorter stand-alone products. They typically address a single issue related to a product or service and include links to more information, including how the reader can purchase the product or request a call from a salesperson.

like the results. If you don't, either edit the file or start over using your own software. Design programs such as Indesign have a built-in print-to-ebook conversion tool that can produce an attractive, functional ebook but it will likely still need some tweaking before you publish it.

Remember that you may want to move some of the material that is part of the front matter in a print book to the back of your ebook. Some ebook distributors will do that for you automatically with certain pages, such as the copyright page. Review every page of your ebook proof before you publish to be sure it looks the way you want it.

Ebooks can include graphics, but style elements such as drop caps (when the first letter of a paragraph has the depth of two or more lines of regular text) or hanging indents (when all of the lines of a paragraph except for the first one are indented) often don't work in ebooks. Keep your text design simple.

A big advantage of ebooks is that they can contain links to other places in the book so readers can move around quickly as well as links to other websites. Be sure to test all your links before publishing.

Another advantage of ebooks is that most e-readers display in color, which means you can use color in the interior at no extra cost. The black-and-white pictures and charts in your print book can be in color in the ebook version. You can also use color for the text but do so conservatively and cautiously. Don't distract the reader with a lot of colored text.

All ebook distributors give you a chance to preview your book as it would look on a variety of e-reading devices before you publish. Use those preview tools and make any necessary changes in your files to give your audience the best possible experience on all platforms.

6

PROTECTING AND IDENTIFYING YOUR BOOK

WRITING A BOOK—EVEN A short one—takes time and effort. If you're going to pour your blood, sweat, and tears into creating a book, you need to know how to protect and identify it.

Copyrights

Ownership of your book is protected by copyright laws. You can find out all you need to know about copyrights at Copyright.gov, but here are some basics to get you started (adapted from Copyright.gov):

Copyright is a form of protection grounded in the US Constitution and granted by law for original works of authorship fixed in a tangible medium of expression. Copyright covers both published and unpublished works, including literary, dramatic, musical, and artistic works such as poetry, novels, movies, songs, computer software, and architecture. Copyright does not protect facts, ideas, systems, or methods of operation, although it may protect the way those things are expressed.

Your work is under copyright protection the moment it is created and fixed in a tangible form that is perceptible either directly or with the aid of a machine or device. This means the idea in your head is not protected; once you write the words down, it is.

You do not have to register your work with the US Copyright Office for it to be protected. However, if you wish to bring a lawsuit for infringement, you will need to register your work. The decision to register your work is up to you. The registration process is simple and easy to do yourself and the cost is nominal. You'll find complete; details and instructions at Copyright.gov.

Names, titles, and short phrases are not copyrightable because they contain an insufficient amount of authorship. Examples of uncopyrightable materials include:

- The name of an individual (including pseudonyms, pen names, or stage names)
- The title or subtitle of a work, such as a book or song
- The name of a character

There may be circumstances under which a name, title, or phrase may be protectable under federal or state trademark laws. You can find out more about that through the US Patent and Trademark Office.

Copyrights are transferrable. Generally, when you sign a contract with a traditional publisher, you will hold the copyright in your name (or the name you choose), and your publishing contract will include a clause that transfers (or assigns) the copyright to the publisher for a specified period of time or set of circumstances. For example, the publisher may retain your copyright while it is actively publishing your book and for a specified number of years after the book is out of print, at which time the copyright automatically transfers back to you. This is what gives the publisher the right to publish your book.

Hybrid and pay-to-publish publishers should address copyrights in their agreements, either to stipulate that you're transferring the copyright to them or that you're not. Read your contracts carefully and understand what they include.

If you decide to transfer your copyright, be sure the agreement stipulates when and how you can terminate that transfer. Expanding on the above example, it's important to know how long you have to wait before you can recover your copyright and publish your book yourself if a traditional publisher takes your book out of print or if sales drop below a certain level. You also want to be clear on what happens to your copyright if the publisher goes out of business.

The copyright notice, which goes on the copyright page of your book, is a statement designed to inform the public that you are claiming ownership of the work. A copyright notice consists of three elements that generally appear as a single continuous statement:

1. The copyright symbol ©; the word "copyright"; or the abbreviation "copr.";

2. The year of first publication of the work; and

3. The name of the copyright owner.

Example: © 2024 John Doe

If someone infringes on your copyright—that is, if they use material from your book without your permission—your first step is to send a cease-and-desist letter which identifies your work, outlines the relevant details of the infringement, and demands that the infringement stop. You can do this yourself or retain an attorney to do it for you. What you do next depends on the particular circumstances such as the severity of the infringement, how much damage it caused, and what, if any, compensation you want.

You need to be aware of copyright laws, but don't obsess over them. Most authors make it through their entire careers without having to deal with a copyright issue.

Your book's identification number

ISBN stands for International Standard Book Number. It's a 13-digit identification number for your book (or book-like product, such as an audiobook); it identifies the book and its publisher. ISBNs are used by publishers, booksellers, libraries, internet retailers, and other supply chain participants for ordering and listing books, as well as for sales and stock control purposes. Each country has an agency designated to assign ISBNs for the publishers in that country. In the United States, that agency is Bowker Identifier Services.

In most cases, as a self-publisher, you'll want to set up a publisher account with Bowker, buy a block of ISBNs (they are sold in blocks of 1, 10, 100, and 1,000), and assign an ISBN you own to your books. Each format or binding must have a separate

You need to be aware of copyright laws, but don't obsess over them.

ISBN (hardcover, paperback, ebook, audiobook, video, etc.). ISBNs are fixed and non-transferable. This means that when you purchase an ISBN, it belongs to you or your publishing company and you cannot transfer it to anyone else. When you assign an ISBN to a book, it's permanently assigned to that book, even if the book goes out of print. You can't reuse an ISBN. ISBNs are not barcodes, although they are used to create your book's barcode.

There are some circumstances when you may opt not to assign an ISBN to a book. For example, if you're not planning to sell your book (perhaps because you're using it as a business promotion tool or you're going to be giving it to family and friends), you don't need an

ISBN. You don't need an ISBN to publish an ebook with Kindle Direct Publishing (Amazon's KDP service); Amazon will assign it a unique 10-digit ASIN (Amazon Standard Identification Number), which will identify the book on Amazon.com.

Many of the online book publishing platforms, including Amazon KDP, Ingram Spark, and Draft2Digital, provide ISBNs at no charge, but the drawback to using their ISBNs is that the platform is shown as the publisher and you can't use the ISBN on a different platform. For example, when you use an ISBN from KDP on Amazon, it shows "Independently published" as the publisher on Amazon. If you use your own ISBN, it will show the name of your publishing company or imprint.

Other self-publishing services also offer free or low-priced ISBNs. Be cautious when using anyone else's ISBN. Remember, the ISBN identifies the publisher as well as the book. If you get your ISBN from any entity other than Bowker in the US (or the authorized agency in the country in which you are located), that ISBN will identify someone else as the publisher. Depending on your publishing goals, that may or may not matter to you; what's important is that you understand it so you can make the right decision before you publish your book.

For more information about ISBNs and to purchase yours, visit Bowker online at myidentifiers.com in the United States or search for the appropriate agency for the country in which you'll be publishing.

An important note about Bowker: Bowker is an affiliated business of ProQuest, which maintains Books In Print®, the leading bibliographic database for libraries, publishers, and retailers around the world. When you purchase ISBNs from Bowker and assign them to a book, the information you submit is automatically included in the Books In Print database and can be accessed by libraries, schools, and retailers.

Barcode basics

If you don't need an ISBN because you're not planning to sell your book or you're only publishing it in electronic format, you don't need a barcode, either. But if you have an ISBN, you should also have a barcode. Barcodes are essential inventory-management tools for booksellers and other retailers, so if your book doesn't have a barcode, retail stores won't carry it. The standard location for a barcode is the lower right corner of a book's back cover.

There are two parts to a book's barcode: the 13-digit ISBN and the retail price, which is shown as a 5-digit number (the first digit indicates the currency and the remaining four digits are the price).

The easiest way to get a barcode for your book is to purchase it for $25 from Bowker after you assign the ISBN. There are a number of ways to get the barcode for free; you'll find several of them at CreateTeachInspire.com/resources.

If you are using Amazon's KDP and do not have

your own barcode, Amazon will add one for you. However, that barcode will be based on Amazon's system, not your ISBN, and will not be useful to any other retailer. If you follow the advice in chapter 7 for publishing your book using both Amazon and Ingram Spark, and you use Ingram Spark's book cover template, it will create a barcode for you at no charge.

Because barcodes are a standard part of book cover design, experienced cover designers can often assist you in obtaining a barcode.

Library of Congress catalog

The Library of Congress (LOC) is the largest library in the world. It's the national library of the United States, the main research arm of the US Congress and the home of the US Copyright Office.

You only need to be concerned with the Library of Congress if you are planning to market your book to libraries. However, self-publishers are not eligible for the LOC's Cataloging in Publication (CIP) program. This program is designed to serve the nation's libraries by cataloging books in advance of publication, and only US publishers who publish titles that are likely to be widely acquired by US libraries are eligible to participate.

The LOC has a program for publishers that don't qualify for the CIP called the Preassigned Control Number (PCN) program. If you are planning to market to libraries, you should secure one of these numbers for your book and include it on the copyright page. It's a fairly simple process, and there is no charge. Details are at loc.gov/publish/prepubbooklink.

7

PUBLISHING YOUR BOOK

W HEN YOUR BOOK IS written, edited, and produced, it's time to publish it. Here's what you need to do:

Set up your publishing company

In chapter 2, I briefly mentioned setting up your own publishing company to make your book look more professional. While it may sound intimidating, it does not have to be a complicated process.

The legal form of your publishing company can be a sole proprietorship, totally owned and operated by you. You can set it up as a corporation or LLC according to the laws of your state, but that isn't essential. Base your decision on your goals for your book and your long-term publishing plans.

The first step in setting up your publishing company

is to name it. You want a name that sounds professional and doesn't obviously connect to you, so don't use your name or initials. Avoid something that sounds like a combination of family names—as much as you adore your kids, grandkids, and pets, don't name your publishing company after them. Also avoid names that could limit what you publish. For example, if you've written a book on business finance, don't name your company Business Finance Books; you might want to write something on a non-finance topic eventually. Avoid using words like *books* in your company name—instead, go with words that will cover a variety of formats, such as *media* or *house* if you feel the need for that type of description.

Once you've decided on a name, check it for legal availability. Exactly how you do this depends on the legal structure you choose. Typically, sole proprietorships and partnerships operating under a name other than that of the owner(s) are required by the county, city, or state to register their fictitious name. Even if it's not required, it's a good idea, because that means no one else can use that name. Corporations usually operate under their corporate name. In either case, you need to check with the appropriate regulatory agency to be sure the name you choose is available.

Next, check to see if anyone is using the name as a website URL. If someone already owns the .com version of your publishing company name, consider coming up with something else. If no one is using the name as a

URL, purchase the domain name as soon as possible. Even though there is an abundance of other URL versions (.net, .org, .edu, .gov, .us, .me, and an almost endless list of specialty terms, including .author), most people still think of .com first when they think of a URL. So if someone is already using yourdomain.com and you decide to get yourdomain.net, you could lose traffic to yourdomain.com if people are typing it in and type ".com" automatically.

Finally, check to see if the name conflicts with any established trademarks. At the state level, your state Department of Commerce can either help you or direct you to the correct agency. You should also check with the trademark register maintained by the US Patent and Trademark Office (PTO).

Once you've decided on a name and checked it for availability, protect it by registering it with the appropriate state agency. If you are anticipating growing into a substantial publishing operation, you should also register the name with the PTO.

After you've named your company, create a logo for it. This doesn't need to be elaborate or expensive, just something distinctive to use on the spine of your books and the copyright page.

If you expect to be selling books directly, such as when you give speeches or participate in other types of events, get a sales tax certificate (also called a resale or resellers permit) from your state. Your state Department of Revenue will explain how to apply and what rules you need to follow in terms of collecting and remitting sales tax. Having a sales tax certificate will allow you to avoid paying sales tax on the books you buy for resale. If you're only going to sell books in third-party online bookstores, such as through Amazon, you don't need a sales tax certificate.

Set up your publishing accounts

With your company name established, you can set up your publishing accounts. These are the accounts you need to produce, publish, and distribute your book. They include:

Bowker. This is the agency we discussed in chapter 6 from which you purchase ISBNs. Visit myidentifiers. com to set up your account and buy a block of ISBNs.

Kindle Direct Publishing (KDP). This is your publishing account on Amazon. You can set up your print and Kindle books here. Visit kdp.amazon.com to get started.

Ingram Spark. Ingram Spark is the indie publishing arm of Ingram Content Group. If you want your books distributed beyond Amazon, you'll need an Ingram Spark account. Go to ingramspark.com; the setup process is similar to Amazon KDP.

An offset printer. If you plan to order large quantities (generally 500 copies or more) of your book, you'll save money by going to an offset printer rather than buying from a print-on-demand or digital printer. There are offset printers that specialize in books both in the US and overseas. To find the right printer for your project, ask your network for referrals, do an internet search, and be a smart consumer by requesting samples and references.

An ebook distributor. The easiest way to get your book on the ever-growing list of ebook sales websites is by utilizing an ebook distributor. You could, of course, open an account with each ebook seller (Apple Books, Barnes & Noble, Kobo, OverDrive, Baker & Taylor, etc.), but it's far more efficient to use a distributor such as Draft2Digital, which is what I use and recommend. Go direct with Amazon by using KDP for your Kindle books, but use a distributor for the other platforms.

Upload your book

When your publishing accounts are set up, you can upload your book. You'll find these services have devel-

Amazon Author Central

Be sure to set up your Amazon Author Central account. Your author page on Amazon is a good place for your readers to learn more about you and see all the books you've written. It's also the easiest way for you to update your Amazon listings and communicate with Amazon about your books.

Amazon encourages you to post a wide range of information on your author page, including your photo, biography, videos, feeds to your blog, events, and more. Learn more about this marketing resource at authorcentral.amazon.com.

oped user-friendly systems that will walk you through the process step-by-step.

Once your book is uploaded, you'll have an opportunity to review an online proof and, in the case of print books, to order a paper proof. I recommend that you always take the time to order and review a paper proof.

KDP Select or not?

Amazon offers an option known as KDP Select, which means you can choose to sell your ebook version exclusively through Amazon. If you go with KDP Select, your ebook could earn higher royalties, and you will have access to certain Amazon promotion tools that non-KDP Select books don't.

The biggest drawback of KDP Select is that you can *only* publish your ebook on Amazon. You won't be able to sell it on other platforms like Barnes & Noble or Apple. For new authors, this may not be a big deal, but for established authors with substantial followings, you could be losing a significant amount of income. Also, if Amazon takes down your book or closes your publishing account for any reason, people have no place to buy your book.

When you choose KDP Select, you are making a three-month commitment. After three months, your book will automatically renew in the program or you can take it out.

A strategy some authors use is to publish a new book in KDP Select for three or six months, then take it out of **KDP** Select and publish the ebook version on other platforms. If you have multiple books, another strategy to consider is to have some of them in **KDP** Select and some not.

KDP Select does not affect where your print books are sold.

Amazon occasionally changes the terms and benefits of the **KDP** Select program. My recommendation is to study the current **KDP** Select features and make a decision based on your particular marketing plans.

Should you make your book available for preorder?

Preorder means that people can buy your book before it's published and it will be shipped when the book is available. Setting up a preorder can generate buzz and help your book hit a bestseller list because advance purchases count toward the book's first-week sales. That means you have weeks or months of promoting your book and building sales that are counted during the book's release week, and that might be enough for your book to rank on a bestseller list.

Another benefit of preorders is to generate new sales from existing readers. You add a link to a preorder page in an existing book so when the readers' appreciation for your work is at its highest (when they've just finished the book), they can preorder the next book. This is especially effective for books in a series.

If you're going to make your book available for

Simple Facts About Self-Publishing

preorder, consider doing it at a discounted price to give readers the incentive to buy it. Also, be sure you can meet your promised publication date.

Preorders tend to work better for well-known authors with established followings, but they could help new authors as well. While you need to know if you're going to offer preorders when you're planning your production and publishing schedule, keep in mind that this is a marketing strategy. Research the process and

If you want bookstores and libraries to carry your book

While books published through KDP are technically available to bookstores, if you're hoping for bookstore distribution, you should also publish your book through Ingram Spark. Amazon competes with bookstores, and bookstore owners are not inclined to purchase their inventory from a competitor. Ingram Spark serves the bookstore and library markets. The best approach is to use Amazon (KDP) for your Amazon sales and Ingram Spark and Draft2Digital for everything else.

Simply having your book available to bookstores and libraries does not mean they will actually carry it. Ingram Spark's website includes information on how to market your book to bookstores and libraries. You'll also want to study more on how to promote your book to these markets because they are distinctly different from online and direct sales outlets.

decide if this is an element you want to include in your marketing plan.

As of this writing, Amazon KDP only offers preorders on Kindle books, not print books. Ingram Spark offers preorder services for print books.

Do you need an audio version of your book?

Digital technology and changing consumption habits are two key reasons the audiobook market is growing at a rapid rate. Should an audiobook be part of your publishing plan? Maybe, maybe not. It's relatively easy to turn your manuscript into a print and ebook designed to be read. It's a lot more complicated (and costly) to turn it into an audiobook that will be heard. Also, while the audiobook market is growing, it's still a small percentage of the overall book market.

The average cost of producing an audiobook runs $400 to $500 per finished hour. That includes narration and editing the audio files. The average person speaks at about 140 words per minute. If you use that as a guide, your 50,000-word manuscript will convert to a six-hour audiobook and cost $2,400 to $3,000 to produce. Longer books will, of course, cost more. If you shop around, it's possible to find audiobook producers who charge less. Also, the more work you give a narrator or producer, the more likely you are to get a reduction in cost. So if you have a backlist (other books you've written), consider negotiating a multi-book deal.

If you feel comfortable recording your book yourself, you can save on the cost of a narrator, but you still need the right recording space (a studio—either your own or one you rent) and the time to do it. You'll also need to learn or hire someone with the technical skills necessary to do the editing and production. Audiobook distributors have strict standards for technical quality.

If your written book is selling well, you may want to consider adding an audiobook. Some experts suggest that if you're selling 10-15 paper copies a day, an audiobook could generate enough additional revenue to make it worth the investment. But if you're barely selling one copy a day, whether it's because no one knows about your book or it doesn't have a broad market, an audiobook is likely to cost significantly more than it will earn.

Here's another thing about audiobooks that makes them frustrating: Unless you're selling them direct to the consumer on your website, you don't get to set the price. You can suggest a price, but the major audiobook distributors make the final decision.

There are a wide range of audiobook production and distribution options, including Amazon's ACX and Author's Republic. A good starting place to research what's involved in creating an audiobook is the Audio Publishers Association, audiopub.org.

8

SELF-PUBLISH YOUR PREVIOUSLY PUBLISHED BOOK

W HY MIGHT YOU WANT to self-publish a previously published book? There are many reasons:

- Your content needs updating and/or expanding.
- Your cover is dull, dated, or just needs freshening up to attract readers.
- You want to change the title.
- You published with a traditional or pay-to-publish company but you're not happy with their performance and you want more control over your book.
- You published with a traditional or

pay-to-publish company in one format and you want to self-publish your book in a different format.

- You published with a traditional or pay-to-publish company that has been sold or has gone out of business.

- You published with a traditional or pay-to-publish company that has taken your book out of print.

The first step in the process of self-publishing a previously published book is to confirm that you own the rights to your book. Check your publishing contract to verify the status.

Traditional publishers typically require you to assign the copyright to them and your contract should outline the circumstances under which the copyright reverts to you. Some pay-to-publish companies specifically state that you own the copyright; others ask for an assignment of some sort.

If your publishing contract says you have maintained your rights, you can move forward with self-publishing your book. If the publishing company owns the rights, you need to get them back. The process of doing this is fairly simple and can be accomplished with what's known as a reversion of rights letter from the publishing company. Your biggest challenge is likely to be getting someone at the publisher to respond to you. Keep badgering them.

How well your book is selling may have an impact on

getting your rights back from a traditional publisher. If your book is selling well, the publisher may be reluctant to let you take it back. If it's not, they may be happy to get it off their list. If you have a literary agent, they may be able to assist you in this process.

Once you have confirmed that you own the rights to your book and you have the production files, you can begin the self-publishing process.

When dealing with a pay-to-publish company, remember that *you* are the customer, and you are choosing to take your business elsewhere (to yourself). You have already paid for your book to be edited, designed, and produced, and you should own all the production files. Ask that they be sent to you so that you don't have to pay for those services again. It's unlikely that a traditional publisher will share those files, but it can't hurt to ask.

What changes are you making?

You may not want to make any changes or maybe just a few small ones to your book, but you want to self-publish it so you have more control over issues such as distribution, pricing, royalty payment schedule, and so on. For example, if you're using your book as a marketing tool, you might be able to save money on the cost of author copies if you self-publish.

If your changes are minor, take the production files you have, make whatever updates are necessary (such as removing the original publisher's information, adding your information, assigning new ISBNs, and making updates to the content), and upload the files to KDP, Ingram Spark, Draft2Digital, and the other online publishing platforms you choose. If the files were created in software you don't have access to or don't know how to use, you'll have to find a freelancer to update the files. Should you be unable to obtain the files, you'll have to recreate them yourself or hire someone to do it for you.

More often, you'll want to make a number of changes, including adding and/or deleting substantial portions of the book's content, creating a new cover, and even changing the title. From the writing and production perspective, approach this in much the same way as you would a new book. Your new content should be well-crafted, edited, and match the style of the original material. You may want to use the existing trim size and interior design, or you may want to change it. At the very least, your cover should be updated to indicate the edition, but you may also want to completely refresh the design so the new edition is clearly distinguishable from the older one.

You're already making changes, so make *all* the changes that could make the new book better. Update your author bio, include QR codes along with spelled out URLs, and add some of the endorsements that you earned after the earlier edition was published.

Once your writing and production work is complete, upload your book to your publishing platforms, check your proofs carefully, and launch your new edition. Be sure to advise the original publishing company that the new book is available and they should remove the older version from their catalog.

Reprints and new editions

According to Bowker, a reprint means more copies are being printed with no substantial changes. You might correct typos, update URLs, and that sort of thing, but essentially it's the same book. If you're using a print-on-demand service, reprints (second and beyond printings) are not relevant.

A new edition means that you have significantly changed the content and it is effectively a new product. You may have added a foreword, new chapters, appendices, and so on. Or you may have removed outdated information. Depending on how much you've changed, you may call this a revised edition or a second edition. This is a subjective decision; there's no hard and fast rule, but a general rule of thumb is that if 30 percent or more of the book is new or updated, it would be a second edition.

Include all previous editions on your copyright page, starting with the most recent.

Updating a book you've self-published

As you move along your self-publishing journey, you're likely to want to update a book you've already published. To correct minor errors and typos, you simply have to upload new files to the publishing platform. To make major changes, you'll follow the same process we've just discussed, except you don't have to be concerned with recovering your rights.

9

CONTENT THAT'S NOT PART OF YOUR MANUSCRIPT

A S WE DISCUSSED IN chapter 5, there is much more to a book than the basic manuscript. Let's take a closer look at a few of those elements.

Cover copy and book description

Your cover copy and the book description you use online are essential sales tools. This is the information that is going to get someone excited about buying and reading your book. You can use the same copy for your back cover as you do for your online description, or you can modify it somewhat. If you don't have the gift of writing marketing copy, consider asking someone who does to help you with this.

The copy on your front cover should include the

title and subtitle of your book and your name (just your name, not "*by* your name"). You may want to include a tag line or something similar to further explain or brand your book. If you have a strong endorsement, especially from someone well-known in your book's target market, you may want to include that on the front cover as well. If your book has won any awards, add an award badge to the front cover.

Your back cover copy can be a description of your book or endorsement quotes or a combination. I've worked with a number of traditional publishers who feel that strong endorsement quotes are best for the back cover copy, but if you go that route, you still need a powerful description for online retailers and wholesalers.

One of the best ways to figure out how to write a good book description is to read a lot of them. Look at bestsellers in your genre and study how the descriptions are constructed. Generally, they will have a headline of some sort designed to draw you in—perhaps a challenging question or attention-getting statement. For non-fiction books, the description should include an overview of what you'll learn and the benefits you'll gain from reading the book. Fiction book descriptions will typically introduce the characters and the plot in a way that makes the reader want to find out more.

Pay attention to the format of your online book description, also known as sales page copy. It needs to be eye-appealing and easy to scan on a screen. One large chunk of text doesn't work—people won't read it. Short paragraphs, headlines, and bullet points are best for online descriptions.

Something all publishers find frustrating is when the bookseller's site drops some or all of the codes after you've uploaded the text with the right attributes (bolding, italics, paragraph breaks, etc.). When that happens, you need to go back and manually correct it. Check the help section on each retailer's site for instructions on how to do it.

Endorsement blurbs for your cover and inside front pages

Endorsement blurbs are those one- to three-line quotes praising your book. You'll often see them on book covers and in the first few pages of a print book under a headline of "Praise for [book title]" or "What readers are saying about [book title]" or something similar. Ideally, they should be from people whose names and/or titles your readers will recognize.

While they aren't essential, endorsement blurbs can be helpful if your prospective buyers are browsing through a lot of books before deciding which one to purchase. People who have given you an endorsement are more likely to help you promote your book. If you decide you need endorsement blurbs, here's how you get them:

Put together a list of people who might be willing to read your book and give you an endorsement for it. When your book is about 95 percent complete, send them a note asking for permission to send them an advance reader copy (ARC) of your book. Here's an example of what to say:

> *My book, [title], is going to be published soon. I would be honored if you read an advance copy and give me a brief quote to use on the cover or the inside front pages. I can send you the book in the format you prefer (pdf, epub, or print) along with some sample quotes to give you an idea of what I'm looking for. I'll need the quote back by [date]. Let me know if this works for you and I'll get the book to you right away.*

How much time you allow for people to read the book depends on the length of the manuscript, but give them at least three to four weeks to read and respond.

Once they say yes, get the book and sample quotes to them. If they've asked for a paper version, mail or hand-deliver a printout. Email the electronic file.

The version you send them can be in manuscript format or designed as it will look when it's published. I prefer to send a designed book for endorsement blurbs; I think it's a more professional approach, but it isn't essential. If you're using a professional designer, find out if they can do this for you and, if so, how much it will add to the cost. Mark the ARC "Uncorrected and unpublished proof provided for review purposes only. Not for distribution to the public."

Provide four or five sample quotes ranging from about ten to thirty words each that represent what you'd like people to say about your book. Take a look at the endorsement blurbs for other books in your genre for ideas.

Ask the reviewers how they'd like to be identified. Business and community leaders typically want their title and organization; an author may ask to include "author of [title]" after their name.

Be clear on your deadline and how they are to respond. For example, "Because of the production schedule, I'll need your quote by [date]. Please email it to me at [email address]."

If the quote they send has misspellings, typos, or clumsy phrasing, correct it and send it back for approval. Most people will appreciate this because it makes them look better—and you don't need to say that's what you've done. Set it up along with their name and credentials as you're planning to use it, and write something like, "Thanks so much for your endorsement. This is how the quote will appear in the book. Please confirm that this is acceptable and that I have your permission to use the quote and your name."

Getting endorsements can be time-consuming and challenging, but this is an important part of book marketing.

When you send someone an ARC and they don't get back with you by the deadline, a gentle follow-up is acceptable. Whether you should nag beyond that is a judgment call you'll have to make based on your relationship and how much you want that person's endorsement.

Not everyone you ask for an endorsement will do it. Some will say no upfront; others may agree to read the book and then fail to provide the endorsement for a variety of reasons; and others will ignore your request. Don't take it personally. When your deadline for gathering endorsements passes, go with what you've got and publish your book. Be sure to send complimentary autographed copies of your published book to the people who provided endorsements.

Foreword

A foreword is an introduction to your book written by someone else. It's not necessary but it can add credibility to your book—and it can be even harder to get than endorsements. If you have a foreword written by someone recognizable and respected by your target audience, you may want to include "Foreword by [name]" in smaller print on your cover.

Getting a foreword can be a challenge, because you are asking that person for a significant amount of time and energy because they need time to read your book and then write an appropriate message. When you request a foreword, be as specific and helpful as you possibly can be. Let the person know why you have chosen them to write the foreword—although you might want to avoid saying, "Because you're famous and I think your name in my book will help me sell more books." Other things you should tell them include:

▤ If there's something in particular you would like for them to include or focus on.

▤ The preferred length if you have one, or if they can write as short or as long as they prefer.

▤ Your production schedule (when you can send the manuscript, when you need their content, when the book will be published).

Offer ways to make the process as easy as possible for them. Give them options of receiving your manuscript digitally or on paper. If they don't have time to read your entire book, provide them with a summary. You might even suggest sending them an initial draft of the foreword that they can modify.

Don't get frustrated or disappointed if the person ignores your request, says no, or says yes and then doesn't follow through. Those things happen in publishing and you just need to deal with it.

Once your book is published, send a signed copy to the person who wrote the foreword.

Disclaimers

A disclaimer is a statement that denies something, especially responsibility. Disclaimers are a way to say, "Don't sue me."

You see them in all kinds of places (on websites, on television shows and movies, at entrances to facilities, in contracts, and in books), serving as a warning to users.

Disclaimers in books are usually found on the

copyright page below the copyright information. This alerts the reader at the outset to whatever you feel is necessary to disclaim. Most book disclaimers are short, typically one to three sentences, but they can be longer if necessary.

In a work of fiction, the author would use the disclaimer to say that the work is a creation of the author's imagination and any resemblance to real people or events is a coincidence. Or that certain places and historical events are real, but the characters and their actions are not.

In nonfiction, authors use disclaimers to establish their expertise or lack of it, to point out that reading the book doesn't establish a relationship between the author and reader, to stress that results are not guaranteed, and to advise readers to seek qualified professional counsel on the subject.

For a memoir or autobiography, the disclaimer could explain that some names and identifying characteristics have been changed, some incidents combined or compressed, and that the work was created based on the author's memory (which may or may not be accurate).

You can also use a disclaimer to warn readers about explicit content, including language, violence, sexual or adult themes, graphic details, and other sensitive topics.

Sometimes publishers, both traditional and pay-to-publish, will include disclaimers saying they are not responsible for the content of the book. They're willing to publish it, but they don't want to be held liable for anything the author wrote.

An internet search on "book disclaimer examples" will yield an abundance of sample language that you can adapt for your disclaimer. Also, it's okay to have fun with your disclaimers. They don't need to be written in boring legalese.

It's important to remember what a disclaimer won't do. A disclaimer is not a license to lie or an excuse for carelessness. It won't stop you from getting sued, and it won't relieve you of liability if your content is intentionally deceptive, misleading, or defamatory, or infringes on someone else's intellectual property rights.

Must you absolutely have a disclaimer in your book? No, but it can't hurt, and it might help if you are the target of a lawsuit.

Beyond the disclaimer that I included on the copyright page of this book, I'm going to stress here that I'm not an attorney, and this section does not constitute legal advice.

10

EBOOKS, SMALL BOOKS, AND OTHER WAYS TO USE BOOKS AS A MARKETING TOOL

I N CHAPTER 1, WE talked about why you should write a book and how books can be a marketing tool for business owners and leaders. If this isn't your motivation for writing a book, skip this chapter. If it is, let's take a closer look at how you can use books to grow your business.

Generate leads with ebooks

Generating quality leads is often one of the biggest marketing challenges for businesses. But what if your prospective customers were willing to pay to receive your basic message and then contact you to tell you they want to know more? That's what happens when ebooks are part of your marketing strategy.

Here's one way that can work:

Write an ebook addressing a key issue related to your product or service. Use the information in chapters 4 and 5 to make sure you've produced a quality book. Because this is going to be an ebook, the length doesn't matter as long as the book covers everything you need to and delivers usable information.

Publish that book as an ebook for sale on Amazon. You may also want to publish it on one or more of the other popular online bookselling platforms. Include links in the book to more information and to a page where readers can either make a purchase or request a salesperson to call (depending on what's appropriate for your product or service).

The result: Your readers have paid to receive your initial marketing message, and when they ask for more information, they're coming to you as a warm lead.

Of course, for this to work, your ebook must have genuine value. It can't just be a brochure or a written sales pitch—it must stand alone as a complete information product. And it must be accurate with no typos or other errors; a sloppy presentation will earn you a bunch of negative reviews which can damage your reputation.

Another way an ebook can work is for you to

produce it in a pdf file and offer it as a free download on your website or social media. You can capture names and email addresses from people who download the file and follow up with them.

Small books can produce big results

If you have information to share that is more than an article but less than a typical 200- or 300-page book, consider writing and publishing a small paperback book.

Small books are exactly that—short books that address a narrow topic. They're typically quick to write and inexpensive to produce. For example, after you've done the writing, editing, and design work, a 30- to 40-page 5"x8" book created from a manuscript of 8,000-12,000 words will cost you about $3 per copy with no minimum print run using a print-on-demand service like KDP.

As a marketing tool, small books are far more powerful than brochures or white papers.

As a marketing tool, small books are far more powerful than brochures or white papers. They establish you as an author and expert in your field. And they're keepers. By that, I mean people are often quick to toss brochures and even giveaways like mugs, but they rarely throw books away. Something else people do with books is they lend or give them to others, which means your book can end up in the hands of people you would never have met. And even though you may create your small book as something you'll give to prospective clients, you can also put it up on Amazon where people can buy it for $5-$10. You may not hit bestseller status, but you'll gain additional exposure and may offset some of your initial costs.

Here are some examples of how small books can be used to market a product or service or to prequalify customers:

- A personal injury lawyer could do a small book focusing on what to do if you're injured in a public place.

- A medical practice could do a small book focusing on certain surgical procedures or health tips, or whatever the practice's specialty is.

- An insurance agency could do a small book on the basic types of insurance every business needs or on what new homeowners need to know about insurance.

- A consultant could do a small book on a narrow part of their area of expertise.

- A product manufacturer could do a small book on how to purchase and/or use their product.

The core of the book should be solid, usable information. You can use a small book to answer the questions you wish your prospects would ask. At the end, include a call to action, such as how to contact you for a consultation or how to purchase your products.

If you have enough material for a small book, you don't have to wait until it's a big book to publish it. And if you have material for several small books, you can create a branded series that you can publish over time and use for different market segments. For example, a law firm could do separate small books on each of their practice areas. A real estate firm could do small books targeted to various segments of their market, such as tips for first-time homebuyers, advice on staging and showing a home for sellers, information on buying investment property, and so on.

You can use small books for lead qualifiers, trade show giveaways, sales call leave-behinds, and a long list of other marketing purposes. Just remember that they are a reflection of you and your company, which means they must be well-written and professionally produced if they're going to generate the results you want.

Other ways your book can work for you

The list of ways to use books in your company's marketing plan is endless. For example, because having a book establishes you as an expert, you can use your book to secure speaking engagements. For the same reason, your book can allow you to connect with media sources so you become their go-to person when they're working on a story in your area of expertise. Use excerpts from your book on your blog—that's called repurposing your content. Depending on your topic, your book might work as a workshop or webinar. You could include it as a "free gift" or bonus with a product purchase.

Thanks to print-on-demand technology, you don't need to buy a lot of copies at once, and you can update the content quickly if need be.

11

OTHER THINGS YOU SHOULD KNOW

T HIS IS THE CHAPTER where I'm putting everything I want to tell you that didn't fit in any
of the other chapters.

Read the bad reviews of other books

Reading reviews of your own books can make you feel
euphoric (if they're good) or send you into the pits of
despair (if they're bad).

Reading reviews of other writers' books can give
you a priceless education about what to do and not do
with your books.

Of course, it's a good idea to check out everything
about an online listing for a competing book. How does
the cover look? How is the description written and
formatted? How are the endorsements and editorial
reviews presented?

But you'll learn the most about what to do and not do with your book when you read the one- and two-star reviews.

For example, we talked about how a book is a great marketing tool to promote yourself and your business, but it needs some useful content as well as your promotional message.

Here are some one-star reviews from a book on self-publishing:

Just a self promo book for the Author...

So did you know [author name] has a blog/webinars? Well buckle up butter cup because about all you will get from this tiny book is basic info and shameless plug to the authors website and multiple webinars. On like every single page. In every single paragraph to where I wanted to throw the book across the room. And most of the tools she says to use for marketing and formatting are quite expensive for the indie author to try. I tried a few things from the book and ended up wasting money on said products that [author name] recommended. If you are interested in said author then just go to her website save yourself the headache.

Don't Waste $

It's primarily a book with links to companies want to sell you something. No real useful instructions.

Use a search engine instead

Everything in this book can be found for free in better-written articles online. A search engine and networking with other authors on social media will help you far more than this book. I suggest you DO NOT get this book, even if you're offered it for free! The author simply wants to entice you to buy into the series of equally disappointing books.

Whatever your book is about, these reviews tell you to limit your self-promotion and be sure your content delivers information the reader can use. Readers who feel like their time and money has been well-spent will be more inclined to respond positively to your marketing message.

The quality of the physical book needs to represent you well. Consider these two-star reviews from a book on investing:

Good book. Poorly printed.

The information in the book is great. The print quality control is no good. Several pages are illegible because the printing is too light to read.

Something wrong with the printing

Many pages are printed with low ink. Hard to see, hard to read.

Be sure you have the necessary quality control measures in place.

Here's a two-star review for a cookbook that retails at $59.99:

poor content

Was expecting better quality books with pictures and better recipes, seems almost childish in their font and design, crummy recipes.

If you're going to charge top-dollar (and even if you're not), you need to deliver top-quality.

Here's a one-star review for a novel:

I'm sorry but a writer should know the difference between ...

I'm sorry but a writer should know the difference between rein and reign. It makes reading the book very difficult when in the third sentence of the first chapter the wrong word is used and then repeatedly used.

And for a different novel:

Who Is Responsible for This Mess?

Not since I read short stories by twelve-year-old authors have I seen so many errors! Who did (or in this case, did not do) the proofreading? Perhaps the proofreader was as drunk as [character name] when he sat in the King Titus chair and did as much damage. Were the time constraints too demanding? The errors get in the way of a potentially beautiful story. This rating is for the proofreader who still has a job to do. Make it right.

Reviews like these are why you need to invest in editing and proofreading.

Of course, not every one-star review is justified. Some readers will leave a one-star review because the shipping was delayed or the package was damaged in transit. That's not fair, but it happens.

Sometimes a book is a target of review bombing, which is when a large number of people leave negative reviews in an effort to damage sales or the author's reputation. You can usually recognize those types of reviews and dismiss them.

Setting those exceptions aside, it's worth your time to study bad reviews in books of every genre and honestly assess whether your book might receive the same criticism. Finding out what readers don't like will help you improve your craft.

Pricing your book

How much should you charge for your book? Let's look at all the issues you need to consider when pricing your book.

Perceived value. People often base their perception of an item's value on its price. If you price your book too low, prospective readers may assume it's not worth much.

Actual value. What is the actual value of your book for your ideal reader? Is it information they can use to improve their lives? Will the information save them money? Is it so many hours of entertainment? Think about what your book will be worth to your readers.

The price of other books in your genre. How much are the popular books in your genre selling for? Be sure you're making an apples-to-apples comparison. If your book is 100 pages, compare it to books of similar length, not ones that are 300-400 pages.

Production cost. For paper versions, what's it going to cost to print your book? Your price needs to cover your costs and allow for a profit. If your goal is to have bookstores carry your book, your retail price needs to allow for your costs, your profit, and a discount for the retailers. Bookstores and gift shops need to make money to stay in business, so most buy books at a 55 percent discount off the retail price to cover their overhead and allow for their profit.

If you have both a paper and an electronic version, your ebook will typically be a few dollars lower than the paper version. If you only have an electronic version without a print book to use as a baseline, you can calculate your price on the perceived and actual value plus the price of similar books in the market.

Even if you're not planning to sell your book because you're going to give it away as a marketing tool, it should have a price on it. That establishes a value for the gift, so you can say, "Get my book worth $XX for free when you sign up for our email list [or do whatever else you're trying to get them to do]" or "A free copy of [book title] by [author name] is included with every purchase—a $XX value!"

Marketing

Marketing books is tougher than ever because there is more competition than ever—and that isn't going to change. As more people figure out how to indie publish, the competition will continue to grow. But because this is a book about the mechanics of self-publishing,

No matter how your book is published, you must market it.

I'm not going to spend any time on book marketing. There are thousands of other resources for you to learn about this topic and I've listed a number of them in the resources list at CreateTeachInspire.com/resources.

Just know this: No matter how your book is published, you must market it. Even established authors published by big traditional houses are doing their own marketing and hiring pricey marketing firms. If you want your book to sell to anyone besides your family members (and, as I've said, most of them will expect free copies), you will have to do the marketing, so do some research and put together a marketing plan.

Organization tips

Writing and publishing a book requires organization. Fortunately, these days you can keep track of everything digitally so you don't need the physical boxes of resources that cluttered my office when I wrote my first books.

It's a good idea to keep all your research and reference materials in case you need to refer to them after the book is published. There are no guidelines for how long you should retain this information like there are for tax returns and other documents, but I recommend keeping it indefinitely.

Another good idea is to keep all drafts of your manuscript; don't simply overwrite your early drafts as you work on your book. Indicate the draft or version number in your file names.

Something that works for me is to create a master document (or a spreadsheet) for the book that includes the key publishing information, such as:

- Book title, subtitle, tagline
- ISBN(s)
- Price
- Descriptions (used for various online sites)
- BISAC codes
- Keywords
- Links to sales sites

This makes it easy to find things quickly if I need to.

How you organize your work process is a personal preference. Do what works for you; just remember that giving it some thought in advance will help your project go more smoothly.

Own where your digital files are stored

Creating, sharing, and storing content in the cloud is mostly safe, but you still should keep backups in a place you own and control. I use Google Drive daily because it's a convenient way to access documents from various devices and share information with others who need it. But I also regularly download those files to my computer's hard drive, which is then automatically backed up to my Backblaze account.

Here's an example of why this is important: A group of romance authors had been writing their manuscripts in Google Docs. Their stories were apparently pretty steamy. When Google realized it, their accounts were shut down because the content violated Google's terms of service. The authors couldn't access their work and they didn't have their files backed up.

Not only did that situation emphasize the importance of redundant backups, it also provides the important reminder to make sure you read and understand the terms of service of any platform you use. When the platform belongs to someone else, the owner (or the lawyers or policymakers) gets to decide what can be stored on their servers. Be sure you know when and why your account could be closed or your data deleted.

Take a look at all the online platforms you use. Set up systems so that if you suddenly couldn't access the information on them, you could still quickly and easily recover that data from one or more backup resources you control.

Hiring professionals to handle all or part of your project

It's unlikely that you're going to want to do everything involved in writing and publishing your book yourself. You may need to hire an editor, a cover designer, or someone to do the interior production. Or you may decide that you want to use a pay-to-publish firm. You'll find a wide range of fees and quality of work among these various providers.

Think ahead of time about how much you want to spend on your book. I know that can be a challenge when you don't have any idea what rates may be—it's that old catch-22 thing that you need a budget but you can't set a budget if you don't know how much things cost. Fortunately, you have the internet to not only get cost estimates but also to find suppliers. I've known people who have had good luck using services like Fiverr, Upwork, 99Designs, and Freelancer—and I know others who treat those sites like poison. You can also ask your friends and colleagues if they know of anyone who provides the services you need. Most of my clients come through personal referrals, although I've had some great ones find me on LinkedIn.

The two most important tips I have for you when it comes to outsourcing book publishing tasks are:

1. Like the person you're going to be working with. Writing and publishing a book can be an intimate process. Especially when I'm ghostwriting, but even when I'm only doing production, I spend a lot of time with my clients. It's important that we be compatible and not have any distracting personality conflicts.

2. Read and understand the contract. This is essential because, among other things, the contract dictates who owns the work. For example, if you hire a cover designer, you want to be sure that you own all the rights to the cover when you pay for it. An indie service provider may not use a formal contract; that's okay as long as you have a clear letter of agreement that covers the important issues such as scope of work and rights. If you use a pay-to-publish firm, you'll find the contracts lengthy and complex. Resist pressure to sign before you've carefully reviewed every clause—and never sign anything you don't understand.

Agreements should be in writing

Always have a detailed written contract when you hire people to provide services for the production and marketing of your book.

Years ago, I went to small claims court and sued a client—who happened to be a lawyer—for non-payment. After some wrangling, we settled with both of us feeling ripped off.

In retrospect, we could have avoided all the ugliness—and perhaps even still be working together—if we had written and both signed a contract that detailed the project and clearly defined what work was included (and not included) in my fee, along with our respective obligations and responsibilities for moving the work forward. But we had exchanged some detailed emails about the project and terms, so when he said he didn't "need" a contract, I let it go. I shouldn't have.

Our primary point of contention had to do with revisions. He retained me to ghostwrite and produce a series of small books; I thought I was clear on how revisions would be handled, but he disagreed. He signed off on the manuscript but wanted additional changes after I had done the production. I told him there would be an additional fee for making the changes and adjusting the design. He got angry, said he wasn't going to pay any more, and threatened to sue me for not completing the project. I decided to go to court before he did. Yes, I sued a lawyer in small claims court. We ended up settling before it went to trial, and I got most of my money. But while it was an interesting experience, it's something I'd rather not repeat.

Insisting on a detailed contract does not indicate a lack of trust. Rather, it provides a vehicle for you to confirm your mutual understanding of your agreement. Contracts don't have to be formal, complex documents (depending, of course, on what they cover); they just have to outline the deal you're making in a way everyone involved understands. This is the chance for you to say, "Wait, that's not what I meant," or "That's exactly what I expect."

Some tips on contracts:

Clearly define the scope of work and fees. Spell out what you are expecting the provider to do and how much you're willing to pay. Define what you'll do if the scope of work changes in the course of the project.

Set fees and payment terms. How much are you going to pay and when are the payments due? Also address the method of payment (check, credit card, online payment service).

Be clear on ownership of intellectual property. Who owns the research, the work in progress, and the final product, and when does the transfer of ownership take place? My agreements clearly state that the project is a work-for-hire, the client owns all the research and other materials, and ownership of anything I create transfers on receipt of the final payment.

> *Insisting on a detailed contract does not indicate a lack of trust. It's a vehicle for you to confirm your mutual understanding of your agreement.*

Make standard provisions apply to both parties. If, for example, the contract exempts the supplier from specific liabilities, the language should exempt the customer as well.

Use precise language. It's difficult to enforce vague language, so be specific. A clause that states a supplier isn't responsible for failures due to causes "beyond the vendor's control" leaves a lot of room for interpretation. More precise language forces a higher level of accountability.

Include a default provision and an escape clause. Describe the circumstances under which either party would be considered in default and what will happen. Also, define what's necessary to terminate the contract if either party wants out.

Include a venue provision. If a disagreement arises that you can't settle amicably and you end up in court, which court will it be? You don't want to find yourself involved in a courtroom battle being waged hundreds or thousands of miles away from where you live. A simple clause that states the location (county), jurisdiction (court), and state law that will apply in the event of a dispute or breach of contract is all you need to keep it local.

Don't assume anything that's not in writing. If it's in the contract, it's enforceable; if it's not in the contract, it's not enforceable. Period.

Consider a legal review. Depending on the amount of money and the degree of risk and liability involved, you may want to have an attorney take a look at your contracts. Remember, I'm not an attorney, and nothing in this book should be considered legal advice.

Tell me about your book

If someone asks you about your book, be able to describe it quickly in a way that will make people want to know more. Come up with a statement consisting of one or two sentences that conveys the genre and theme of your book.

For example, my book *Christian Business Almanac* is a page-a-day resource for Christian businesspeople who want to be able to integrate their faith with their work lives. My novel *Choices* is contemporary fiction that opens with a hit-and-run crash and follows the driver and the victim as they work through the aftermath of the accident and come to eventual resolutions. My inspirational book *Finding Joy in the Morning* is a guide for helping people find peace and get through tough times.

Develop similar descriptions for your book so that when someone says, "Tell me about your book," you can do it quickly. Of course, also be ready to tell them more if they ask.

Don't rush

You may have seen ads for "create your book in three days" programs and other promotions to get your book written and published quickly. Or you may be tempted to speed through the publishing process because you're excited and want to feel your book in your hands. Don't! Take your time and do everything you need to do to produce a quality book.

Book printing tip

You may want to have a relatively small number of books for a narrow market printed, and you've thought about taking them to a quick printer or office supply store. If you do that, you not only have to pay to have the copies printed and bound, but you also have to deal with fulfillment (packaging and shipping) when you sell them. If you publish them through Amazon KDP, you can order the exact number of books you want (from one to 999 copies) and let Amazon handle printing and fulfillment. You can order more at any time and have them delivered in a matter of days, so you don't have to store large quantities of them. And when it's easier, you can send people who want to buy them to Amazon instead of handling the physical book yourself.

You can also order author copies at a competitive per copy price through Amazon and have them sent to other people. You have to pay for shipping and you don't earn a royalty on author copies, but there may be situations where this works for you. For example, I have clients who like to give away some of my books to their prospects and they order 20-50 copies at a time from me. The clients pay me for the books and I have Amazon print them and ship them directly to wherever my clients want to receive them—it's a simple, no stress way to handle it.

The practical reason for traditional publishing seasons

The large traditional publishers have historically had two publishing seasons: spring and fall. It's the time when they publish their catalogs and make new books available. Bookstore buyers have long been accustomed to incorporating this into their purchasing schedules. If you work with one of those publishers, every part of your book's production schedule will be linked to getting it in one of those catalogs.

I used to think that these seasons were based on consumer buying habits, but it wasn't anything so scientific—it was simply nature. When the Erie Canal opened in 1825, it allowed New York publishers to send books to the interior of the country on boats, which was the most efficient way to ship those heavy objects. But the canal froze in the winter, forcing publishers to ship books before and after the freeze. The "Spring list" and "Fall list" became the industry standard.

Of course, with the availability of motor freight and printing facilities all over the world, publishers' dependence on the Erie Canal gradually declined, although many continued the tradition of spring and fall publishing seasons. Today, the Erie Canal is mainly used by recreational watercraft.

Thanks to modern transportation, publishers don't have to consider issues like freezing weather, although traditional publishers still produce semi-annual catalogs. As an indie publisher, you can publish your books when they're ready, but you shouldn't totally ignore seasonal issues. When you schedule the release of your books, consider the buying habits of your audience as well as the operational requirements of the retailers. For example, if your goal is to have your book in bookstores and gift shops for Christmas, it needs to be available in late summer or early fall before the buyers have completed their holiday orders.

Avoid scams

The rapid growth of self-publishing has contributed to the proliferation of self-publishing service providers—and scammers. Common industry scams include companies that charge you for services that are free or almost free, try to sell you worthless marketing packages, encourage you to enter meaningless contests with a substantial entry fee, get you to pay for bogus reviews, and more—and their sales pitches are quite persuasive.

How can you avoid scams and poor quality operators?

One way is to ask other indie authors for recommendations, but whether you find a source through a referral or an internet search, do your due diligence. No matter how good the presentation is or how much you like the person, research the company or individual to determine if they have the skills you need. Ask about their history. How much experience do they have working on projects similar to yours? Get and check references. Ask to see samples of their work. Ask to review their contracts. Conduct an internet search to see if any complaints surface. If you find poor reviews, evaluate them for fairness before making a final decision—after all, even the best of companies has the occasional unhappy customer.

Another excellent way to protect yourself against

scammers is to read chapter 13, "Avoiding Scams and Myths," of Helen Sedwick's book, *Self-Publisher's Legal Handbook*. Sedwick is an author and business attorney, and her book contains a wealth of information written in an easy-to-understand and entertaining style. You'll find a link to *Self-Publisher's Legal Handbook* under the "Recommended Reading" section at CreateTeachInspire.com/resources.

Most important: Remember the adage if something sounds too good to be true, it probably is.

Should you borrow money to publish your book?

Many publishing pay-to-publish companies offer financing to "help" authors get their books published. Should you go into debt to publish your book? It is, of course, your choice, but my advice is: No.

Sometimes this is a loan provided by a third-party company. As an alternative, most publishing companies accept credit card payments for their services. And you may think you can borrow this money now and pay it back with royalties when your book sells.

But what if your book doesn't sell enough copies to cover the cost of publishing?

In chapter 3, we talked about preparing a business plan for your book that would include the expenses involved in publishing and marketing, as well as the revenue the book can realistically be expected to generate.

Let's say it's going to cost $5,000 (a conservative

estimate) for you to have your manuscript edited, your cover designed, your interior designed and produced, and for all the other essential details that have to happen to get your book published. The publisher explains that you'll earn $3 a copy on retail sales. That means you're going to have to sell more than 1,600 copies to break even on the publishing costs without factoring in marketing, advertising, and other expenses. Maybe you'll earn $5 a copy. That still means you need to sell 1,000 books to break even on just the production cost.

According to Steven Piersanti, senior editor with Berrett-Koehler Publishers:

> *The average book published today is selling less than 300 print copies over its lifetime in the US retail channels. Even if e-book sales, audio sales, sales outside of the US, and sales outside of retail channels are added in, the average new book published today is selling much less than 1,000 copies over its lifetime in all formats and all markets.*

Will your book beat the average? It could happen, but should you risk going into debt on that chance?

Let's be clear on this: If you have the money and want to spend more on publishing your book than you can expect to earn from it, that's fine. It's your choice. I have worked with many clients over the years who tell me that they know their book is not likely to generate a profit, but they believe in their message and they can afford the cost. They say things like, "If it helps just one person, it's worth it."

My business clients see the cost of their books as a marketing expense for their companies. The revenue from book sales is incidental compared to the benefit the company receives from the owner being a published author.

But if you don't have the disposable cash to pay for the cost of publishing, think long and hard about taking a loan or using a credit card to fund your book. And remember that pesky detail of the interest lenders charge. If you borrow money to publish your book, you'll end up paying back substantially more than the actual cost of publishing.

What's the alternative to going into debt to publish your book? One way is to figure out how to do as much of the production process as possible yourself. Another is to try to raise money through crowdfunding platforms like Kickstarter. You can look for other ways to share your message, such as blogging and online videos.

Don't let fulfilling your dream of publishing a book turn into a burden of debt that you may not be able to repay.

12

WHAT NOW?

I HOPE YOU REALIZE THAT independent publishing is a powerful tool that can help you reach a variety of goals if you are willing to do the work.

My goal for this book was to take the mystery out of self-publishing and show you how to do it yourself or hire others to do it for you without getting ripped off. If you've made it this far and you still want to write and publish a book, great.

Several years ago, I launched a series of books called *Conversations*. Most of them were short ebooks on a narrow topic created from edited interviews with experts. One was *Get Your Book Published*, based an interview with self-publishing consultant and editorial project manager Marla Markman. As I've mentioned, an updated version of that ebook is included in this book as Appendix 1. It expands on much of the information I've shared about the various types of publishing and how to decide what's best for you, how to find self-publishing resources, and more. I encourage you to read it before you start putting together your book plan.

If you're thinking about using a pay-to-publish company, check out Appendix 2. It's a list of questions you should ask before you sign a contract. This information started out as an article for my blog and expanded into an ebook.

The resources section at CreateTeachInspire.com/resources gives you details on the resources I use and recommend.

The Glossary defines many of the terms used in this book and, for some of them, includes links for more information.

So, as the chapter title says, what now? It's up to you, of course, but here's what I think:

The world needs your book—get it out there.

APPENDIX 1

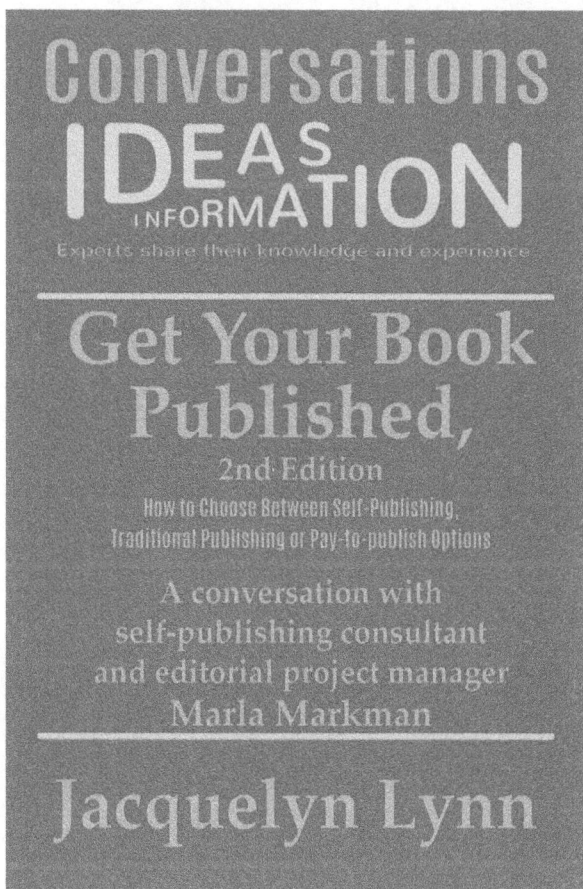

Conversations
IDEAS
INFORMATION
Experts share their knowledge and experience

Get Your Book Published,
2nd Edition
How to Choose Between Self-Publishing,
Traditional Publishing or Pay-to-publish Options

A conversation with
self-publishing consultant
and editorial project manager
Marla Markman

Jacquelyn Lynn

*This book was last updated in 2019. Some company
names and other information may have changed, but
the core information is still valid.*

INTRODUCTION

JACK CANFIELD AND MARK Victor Hansen came up with the idea of *Chicken Soup for the Soul* in 1993. The two were motivational speakers and the book was a compilation of the best 101 stories they told in their presentations. That first *Chicken Soup* book has sold more than 11 million copies and spawned the best-selling trade paperback series of all time, with more than 250 titles.

But when Canfield and Hansen first presented their idea to New York publishers, they were turned down by every one of them (some stories say more than 100 publishers rejected the book). Finally a small Florida-based health and wellness publisher decided to give the book a chance.

Today, Canfield and Hansen might have skipped the trip to New York or at least stopped pitching to publishers at the first couple of rejections and instead published the book themselves.

If you're looking to add "published author" to your credentials, you have more options than ever. But all those options can be confusing, and making the right choice so that you can create a quality book that will help you achieve your goals without getting ripped off depends on a number of variables. I sat down with self-publishing consultant and editorial project manager Marla Markman to get the information you need to choose the path to publication that's best for you. Because this is such a rapidly-changing industry, we recently talked again to update and expand this guide.

Marla is a publishing professional and award-winning editor with 30 years of experience creating, editing, and managing nonfiction content for a wide range of media, from magazines and books to websites and marketing collateral. I first got to know Marla when she was with Entrepreneur Press, the book publishing arm of the media company that publishes *Entrepreneur* magazine. Marla was instrumental in launching the company's trade book division, where she acquired, developed and edited many top-selling books, including more than a dozen of mine. She left Entrepreneur in 2008 to create Markman Editorial Services and fulfill her own entrepreneurial dream.

In *Get Your Book Published*, Marla walks you through the traditional and self-publishing processes, pointing out the advantages and drawbacks of each so that you can make the decision that is best for you.

Something that makes both Marla and me angry is the increasing number of companies out there that offer publishing services but are more interested in separating authors from their money than in producing quality books that authors will be proud of and consumers will want to buy and read. We spent a lot of time talking about how to identify and avoid those companies. We also talk about how to find legitimate, high-quality service providers that will help you produce a book you'll be proud of.

Are you ready to find out how to get your book published? Let's dive in.

Jacquelyn Lynn

WHY PUBLISH A BOOK?

JL: *Before we get into the specifics of how to get a book published, let's talk about why knowing how to do it is important. Who is likely to want to know how to get a book published and why should they want to publish a book?*

MM: Most people who are getting books published these days are coaches, entrepreneurs, business people, CEOs—anyone who wants to establish themselves as a thought leader. Having a book immediately establishes your credibility, which could generate more business and speaking opportunities.

In my business, I deal with a lot of coaches—wellness coaches, leadership coaches—and people who want to build up their speaking careers, such as motivational speakers, that type of thing. It's important for them to have books.

The other class of people that would want to publish a book would be fiction writers. There have been many success stories of fiction books that are selling like gangbusters because they're inexpensive to produce and sell, and can be easily churned out once you have a successful formula.

JL: *Like* Fifty Shades of Grey? *It started out as a self-published ebook.*

MM: Yes, like *Fifty Shades of Grey*. There are a lot of self-published books that are like that, both fiction and non-fiction, that are success stories, that have done really well. Some of them have done so well that traditional publishers have picked them up. I have clients who were picked up by traditional publishers after self-publishing.

JL: *Is there another category of author who might be interested in getting a book published?*

MM: I'm not sure if you want to call this a separate group, but memoir writers are a big group. A memoir can be non-fiction, a hybrid of non-fiction and fiction, or it can be completely fictionalized but you're basing it on your story. You might have a memoir that you use to establish your credibility or as a self-help book, like if you're writing about how you got over a tragedy in your life. You can turn that experience into a book that you can use to get speaking opportunities. However, even though having the book out there may give you credibility, in general memoir books are very difficult to sell.

JL: *Because if you're not famous, who cares about your story?*

MM: Right. You have to have a very compelling transformation story for anybody to care.

JL: Of course, if you just want to put your story down on paper for your family, you could write your memoir and publish it. You shouldn't expect a whole bunch of strangers to buy it, but the story is recorded.

MM: There are a variety of reasons why you'd want to create a memoir. If you're not interested in or don't need to have sales and you just want to write it for a legacy for your family is one reason. Obviously you can't expect it to sell a great deal. But that's okay, if that's what your mission is. Or, as I've said, if you have a compelling story and you want to use that to get consulting or speaking engagements, writing and publishing your memoir is an effective way to do that.

THE STATE OF PUBLISHING

JL: Your career as an editor began with a traditional publisher. How has the industry changed since "back in the olden days"?

MM: Back in the olden days when we had David Hasselhoff in a hot tub on the cover of *Entrepreneur*. [Laughing]

JL: Yes, back in those days. But seriously, I'm talking about back in the days when the only way to get a book on the market was to get a contract with a traditional publisher, and that was difficult. How have you seen the industry change for the three major groups: authors, publishers and readers?

MM: Like you said, when I worked for a publisher, really the only way to get a professional quality book was through a traditional publisher or perhaps through a good vanity press, which we'll talk about later. And a vanity press was cost-prohibitive for many people and it also had a negative connotation attached to it. But the difference is now it's easy for virtually anyone to produce a quality book that reads and looks like any one that's been published by a traditional publisher.

That's why, like you said earlier, there are so many books now like *Fifty Shades of Grey*, that have become bestsellers and even movies, even though they began as a self-published book.

For readers, the industry has changed as well, in large part because of the advent of inexpensive ebooks, they are as little as 99 cents, and e-readers [Kindle, Nook, iPad, tablets, smartphones], which are becoming very pervasive. In some cases, ebooks are selling more than traditional books. And audiobooks are huge now. The growth in audiobooks is out-pacing ebooks. It's easier and cheaper than ever for readers to get the books that they want and consume as many as their time allows.

JL: One of the more interesting trends in publishing is the growth in audiobooks. How is this affecting the industry in general and indie publishers in particular?

MM: It is making it so that you have another channel to offer your potential buyers. Audiobooks have grown tremendously and they are actually surpassing the sales of e-books.

JL: In total sales or in growth?

MM: Both. The last statistic that I read is they have grown by 30 percent in sales and readership. I always encourage my clients to produce an audiobook because I think the more formats your book available in, the better. People are responding more to audiobooks because they can listen to them anywhere while they are doing other things, like commuting or working out. Audiobooks are not as inexpensive as ebooks, but the potential for sales is good.

JL: Back to the industry in general. I've heard that traditional publishers are hurting.

MM: I don't think that traditional publishers are really hurting. Yes, they are competing with self-publishers, but there will always people who want to publish through traditional publishing. And as we'll talk about later, a lot of them have started their self-publishing arms. The only group that is hurting in the industry is the bookstores.

JL: That's primarily because of ebooks and buying on the internet, right?

MM: Right. It's so easy now for people to buy books off the internet that not many people are going into the bookstores anymore. When I worked at Entrepreneur, it was even happening then. We were having to think of non-traditional means to gets our books out there. That's when we started thinking of selling on the internet or going into different places other than traditional bookstores. Like, we started selling to Costco and Office Depot and any place where you could get your book out there because bookstores were just going by the wayside.

JL: I'm an avid reader, but I rarely go into bookstores, and usually it's to do research.

MM: I still go into bookstores. Even though they're waning, I think there will always be bookstores, they just won't be as popular as they were. People are saying that print will die at some point, but it's never going to, because there are people who will always like the feel of a book in their hand.

Another thing that's changing is that the variety of books is wider than ever. Authors are targeting niche markets. Also, most readers don't care or probably don't even realize when they're reading a self-published book. Because if it's done correctly, if you take the time and the investment to produce it correctly and get a high-quality book, nobody's ever going to know it was self-published. It could compete with a book that's traditionally published. Readers just care about the content. They just want it to be entertaining or helpful or whatever they're looking for.

THE PRIMARY PATHS TO PUBLISHING

JL: Before we talk about the primary paths to publishing, let's clarify some of the terms we'll be using. The term "self-publishing" has been around for a long time, but in recent years, the terms "indie publishing" and "independent publishing" are becoming more common.

MM: Indie and independent publishing are the same thing. The Independent Book Publishers Association (IBPA), the biggest association in this industry, is trying to get people to use "independent publishing" instead of "self-publishing" because it sounds more professional. They're trying to level the playing field between traditional publishers and people who publish their own books.

Something the IBPA offers that I recommend every author review is the Industry Standards Checklist for a Professionally Published Book. You can download it here: https:// www.ibpa-online.org/page/standardschecklist.

JL: So when we talk about the primary paths to publishing, the two big umbrellas are traditional publishing and self-publishing or independent publishing. Let's talk about the key similarities and the key differences.

MM: There are actually *three* primary paths. There's traditional publishing, there's self-publishing, and then there's hybrid publishing which combines elements of both.

The key similarities are book quality and marketing. You will end up with a professional quality book if you're a savvy self-publisher. I want to emphasize that means you have to do everything professionally—get a professional editor, a designer—and if you do that right, your book is going to look just like a book that was traditionally published by one of the major houses. The other similarity is marketing, because all books are going to need to be marketed and promoted if you're going to sell them—whether you have a publisher backing you or not.

JL: Even when a major publisher takes on your book, a lot of people think, "Okay, all I have to do is write the book, and then I can go do something else because the publisher will market it," and that's not true.

MM: You're right. Unless you're an A list author, and by that I mean the established authors with track records that the publishers know sell well over time, publishers are going to put your book out and it's only going to be on the shelves for about six weeks, and that's all the time you have to really market your book. The publisher is only going to do a minimal amount of marketing. Once the six weeks is done, if they haven't sold very many copies, your book is just going to get remaindered. That's when you go into the bookstores and you see the books that have the big price discount stickers on them, that have been slashed to $5 or whatever, those are remaindered books. That's all the chance you get to market and sell your book with a traditional publisher.

JL: What are some of the key differences between self-publishing, traditional publishing and some of the hybrid publishing models?

MM: From the author's perspective, the key differences are risk, cost, distribution and time to press. It's riskier to spend the money yourself with no guarantee of a return on investment. If you go through a traditional publisher, they are going to pay you an advance and then they foot the bill for everything else. Obviously, it's more expensive to self-publish because you have to pay for everything. However, even though you're taking on the risk and putting in all the investment, the good thing is that if everything goes well and you market your book well and it does well, then the payoff is also higher if you self-publish than if you go with a traditional publisher because you get all of the profits.

Another difference is that if you go through a traditional publisher, you'll have a wider distribution because they have more access to distribution sources. It's difficult for a self-publisher to get into a lot of the big retail distribution areas. It's hard to get into bookstores, sales reps won't take on a self-publisher who only has one book. There are ways to get around that, but it's more difficult.

Of course, time to press is a big difference. If you're doing it yourself, you can get it done in four to six months, versus a year or more if you traditionally publish.

JL: What about hybrid publishing?

MM: Hybrid publishing is a basically a pay-to-publish model. You pay to publish your book, but you receive royalties on the sales when you're book is published. Hybrid publishing is also called partnership publishing, it's a shared risk. You go through a curated, collective acquisitions process—they have to approve your book before they'll take it on. You're paying for it, but they do all the production and some of the marketing for you. With hybrid publishing, you're supposedly going to be in a more exclusive class of books than self-publishing because of the acquisitions process. Another benefit is that the publishers may be able to get your book reviewed by prestigious publications like *Publisher's Weekly* and *Library Journal*. Again, a self-publisher can do this, but it's a lot more difficult for them because they don't usually have the connections.

JL: So with hybrid publishing, if the book flops, both the hybrid publisher and the author lose. If it's successful, they both make money. It's not like in straight self-publishing, where you have a printer who charges you X dollars for Y number of books, and the printer doesn't care if you sell the books or not. The more books you sell with the hybrid publisher, the better for everybody involved.

MM: Exactly. You and the hybrid publisher will share in the profits from the book. More and more companies are taking this model, but it's a case of buyer beware. There are some really great ones out there, like She Writes Press is really good, but there are some really bad ones out there, too.

JL: Describe how traditional publishing works today.

MM: Today, to be traditionally published, you need several things. A traditional publisher or an agent will want to see a track record or at least an established author platform. To be published by one of the major houses, like Simon & Schuster or McGraw Hill, you need an agent. To get an agent, you need to write a proposal and a query letter. A proposal is usually around 30 pages and we could have a whole book just about that. Briefly, it includes two sample chapters, table of contents, a description of every chapter, a competitive analysis, your background and experience, and your marketing and promotion plan. It could take up to a year or more to get an agent who believes in your book enough to want to try to pitch it to a publisher. Once you have the agent, that's just the beginning. Because then it can take up to a year or more for an agent to convince a publisher to take on your project.

Many publishers will even want to see that you have preorders from established contacts, and marketing and publicity tours and interviews already set—it's getting more and more difficult to have a traditional publisher take you on if you're an unknown because the risk for them is so great.

Once your book has been purchased by a publisher, they

will pay you a small advance to finish writing your book and then it goes into production. The lead time from there is typically about a year. Once it's published, you'll get royalties based on a percentage of the sale price of the book. The more books that are sold, the more royalties you get. Typically, there's a tier—the more books you sell, a lot of times the royalty rate will go up.

As we said before, the problem is, unless you're an A list author, then you only get about six weeks for the publisher to see how your book is going to perform, and they'll just do the basics when it comes to promotion. You need to actively promote the book yourself.

Another drawback to traditional publishing is in most cases, the traditional publisher is going to have the final say over the title and design of your book. You'll have input, but they're going to make the final decision. So if you want ultimate control over your book, self-publishing is the better way to go.

JL: Describe how self-publishing works.

MM: With self-publishing, you write the book, of course. You get it edited, then get the cover and interior designed, have it proofread, indexed and then write the back cover copy. Along the way, you're also going to need to get an ISBN and CIP code, which is what gets you into libraries if you want to go that route, and a bar code. Those are the basics. Then once it's produced, you could choose to either upload your files to a print-on-demand service like Kindle Direct Publishing (KDP), which is the self-publishing arm of Amazon, or IngramSpark, which the self-publishing arm of Lightning Source. The beauty of print-on-demand is that you only have to print the number of copies you need, so you don't have to worry about storing thousands of books in your garage.

Print-on-demand is another reason why today is such a great time to be a self-publisher, because before print-on-demand existed, you had to go to what is called an offset printer. With an offset printer, in order to get the unit price down to a reasonable amount, you would have to print thousands of copies of your book, and then you would have to store those in your garage or pay to have them stored in a warehouse. With print-on-demand, you only print the number of copies that you need.

JL: One of the cool things about print-on-demand is that because you're only having them printed as they're ordered, if you find a mistake, you can easily correct it for future copies. Also, if you go with Kindle Direct Publishing and Amazon, the paper book is listed on Amazon and KDP prints it when it's ordered. So people can buy it online and you don't ever have to touch it.

MM: Right. The per-unit price is higher for print-on-demand, but you don't have to order thousands of books at a time, so that makes up for the higher price. And it's still, of course, lower than the retail sales price.

I work with a lot of clients who do a combination of print-on-demand and offset. They do print-on-demand because they want it listed on Amazon so they can direct people to Amazon from their website and people can buy single copies there. But they also do offset when they need a large number of copies. For example, I work with a lot of speakers. If they're speaking to an association or an organization that they can get to pre-order copies for all of their members, then they use the offset printer to fulfill that order.

With an offset printer, if you plan on printing anything over 500 copies, then you can get the per-unit cost down to a reasonable price. It's going to be economical. But anything under that is not worth it to do offset. So a lot of people are doing both.

Back to how the process works: Once you've uploaded your book to a print-on-demand or offset printer, you would want to get it converted into an ebook and then you would need to choose a distributor for that. Most people typically have it distributed through Amazon's Kindle. The two main ebook formats are mobi and ePub. Kindle, which is available only available through Amazon, uses mobi. The other ebook platforms—iBooks, Nook, Kobo, Google Play and others— use ePub. If you want to get it into iBooks and other than Amazon platforms, there are lots of distributors you can go with. Draft2Digital and BookBaby are two big ones. Or you could go to Smashwords. There are a lot to choose from.

Then the hard part comes, which is marketing. When you self-publish, it's all on you. You can either do it all yourself, which a lot of people do, or you can hire a marketing firm or a publicist to do it for you. It's not anything that's difficult, you just have to know what to do and it takes an investment of your time. The great thing is the more books you sell, the more money you make. You don't have to share profits with anybody, a hybrid publisher or traditional publisher.

Like I said before, there are a lot of self-published books that have done so well, they've been picked up by a traditional publisher. I just had a client who was able to get her book featured in the *New York Times*, and she did that all herself without a publicist. But she was very diligent and very aggressive in her marketing. Because of that, an agent found her and wanted to represent her. So it is possible.

JL: You've mentioned more than once that a traditional publisher could pick up your book if you self-publish and you're successful. I know that happens. But if you're a successful self-publisher, why would you go with a traditional publisher and get 15 percent instead of 100 percent by self-publishing?

MM: That's a good question, and I think that's part of what we're talking about here. There are people who do both— they self-publish some books and traditionally publish others. There are people only do self-publishing. Their logic is: Why would you go with a traditional publisher if you want all the control, you want all the profits? But there are some people who still think that being published by a traditional publisher is the ultimate, the coup de gras. This one particular author that I've talked about, she has a book called *The Joy of Financial Security*, and she's done very well. She was reviewed in *Kirkus*, which is one way to get a lot of people to see your book. And she's been reviewed in the *Wall Street Journal* and the *New York Times*. Her book has done really well. But she said that she still wants that cred of being able to say that she was published by a traditional publisher. So for her next book, she's seeking traditional publishing.

Some people just want to be able to say, "I was published by a traditional publisher," because they think, even though you could still make more money self-publishing in this day and age, traditional publishing still has that credibility.

JL: So it depends on what your goals are.

MM: Exactly. When we were talking about the pros and the cons—a lot people think their route to getting to a traditional publisher is self-publishing and doing it really well. In the case I just mentioned, because she had an agent come to her after her book did really well, and the agent said, "I want to do your next book with you, and I'm going to promote it to X traditional publisher," she was able for her next book to cut the usual time to market in half. Because if she had started from the beginning, from where she had been a nobody and didn't have this established credibility with this self-published book that had done really well, she may never have got that agent, or it would have taken her a lot longer. She cut that advance time in half.

I think that's appealing as well. Some people, even if they think that, okay, maybe I can convince a traditional publisher and agent to take me on, they just are antsy and they don't want to wait.

JL: I have found this with my clients in the past. I've explained how long the traditional publishing route takes, and that you may or may not be able to get a traditional publisher to take your book, but even if you do, it's going to be two to three years from the time you start to look for an agent and do everything else until you have a book on the market. But if you go the self-publishing route, in six months, you can have a book on Amazon and in readers' hands. A good book. And most of the time, they choose to self-publish.

MM: I had another client who had a book—it's about age-proofing your home, the name of the book is *Staying Power: Age-Proof Your Home for Comfort, Safety and Style* by Rachel Adelson—and her book also did really well. She's been approached by a traditional publisher to publish her book. It's easier for her to do that now because they approached her, and that wasn't even an agent, that was the actual publisher. So now she's cut out a huge part of that waiting time.

JL: *Since you mentioned hybrid publishing, explain the process. How does it work?*

MM: With hybrid publishing, you still have to give them some sort of proposal. It doesn't have to be as extensive as if you were trying to get an agent or a traditional publisher. A lot of times, hybrid publishers, like Greenleaf Book Group or Motivational Press, are very aggressive in approaching authors. If they see an author or they see a businessperson—I've even gotten approached by some of those companies if they see that I'm a successful entrepreneur—they'll approach you, and say, "Hey have you ever thought about writing a book, we can help you do that." Or if they see somebody who is doing really well as an author, same thing. They say, "We can help you." Greenleaf has a great track record creating bestsellers. They'll say, "We can help you do even better than you already are."

If you approach a hybrid publisher, you submit to them similarly to how you'd submit to an agent or a traditional publisher. You give them a proposal and they either say your book is good enough for us to publish or it's not—pretty much like a traditional publisher.

From that point on, the production process is essentially the same as being with a traditional publisher. Hybrid publishers often offer different packages which include editing, design and other services. You have to be really careful because some of these companies will have add-on packages. For example, the original deal might not include marketing. I've worked with some authors who didn't realize that that their hybrid publisher agreement didn't include marketing, so they either had to end up doing it all themselves, or they had to pay for a very expensive marketing package as an add-on. There are a lot of hybrid publishers that are very good and they're legitimate, but not all of them all, so you have to beware and know the right questions to ask.

JL: What's the difference between a hybrid publisher and subsidy publishing?

MM: Subsidy publishers really don't want to sell your book. They just want to take money from you. Whereas a hybrid publisher, in my eyes, is more respectable, has a better reputation, and their goal really is to be a partner with you.

JL: It used to be pretty simple—you either went with a traditional publisher or a vanity press, and you paid the vanity press to produce your book. But now there are so many combinations and types of companies offering publishing services.

MM: There are so many permutations of publishing. There are also a lot of agents who are starting their own self-publishing services. That's called agent-assisted publishing. There are agents who find books that they believe in that they can't find a traditional publisher for, so they are offering publishing packages to the authors. They haven't been around enough for me to know how well that's doing. It's a relatively new method. But I know that is becoming more and more a way that books are getting published.

There's also what they call author-assisted publishing. That could either be a subsidy publisher, where you buy a package, and it could pricey and it could be a ripoff, but it might not be. That's where they edit the book for you and you get a percent of each sale. That method could even include

Kindle Direct Publishing, Lulu Press, or Bookmasters. There are a lot of companies that will offer to design your book and you can either buy the whole package or you can buy it ala cart.

Some of them are fine. Some of them do good work. But have to know how much you're paying for things and make sure to look at the quality. Because sometimes the quality is not there. But sometimes it is. You just have to be careful.

JL: Do your homework.

MM: Yes. I had an author who, as much as I tried to talk him out of it, he had his book designed by [a well-known ebook publisher]. I don't think it cost him much for the design. Initially he only did it as an ebook, and that book won an award. It's called *Mystic Witness* by Larry Alboher. He actually won a global ebooks award, which was through Dan Poynter's organization.

JL: Sounds like he got lucky.

MM: He was really lucky that he ended up with a good product. Overall, if you want a sure thing, you should go with an established entity with a strong reputation that you know is going to do a good job. You want a designer who has a great reputation, that only designs books and not all kinds of other material, who will not treat you as a number and will give you individual advice and consult with you, rather than going to a low-cost service where they may once in a while do a really great job. And that may cost you more than some of the high-profile, low-cost services.

JL: It's not always price, you have to make sure you're getting quality. If you're on a limited budget, you still have to do some serious evaluating of your resources.

MM: That's it. A big benefit of being a self-publisher is that you have that control over every part of your product. I think if you really want to make sure you get the best quality book, you will exercise that at every step. When you go to a company like a KDP or a BookBaby, you're not going to get the individual attention. I think it's best for people to avoid assembly line type situations. Otherwise you're losing part of that control. Even though it seems like you have it, you're really losing part of it.

JL: I've not worked with BookBaby, so I don't know how they operate. But I have published books through KDP for myself and for clients. All they do is the print the book and make it available on Amazon, and they've always done a good job. You need to understand exactly what services they're providing.

MM: Right.

JL: You also need to understand your contract and refuse to accept a low-quality product. Back when traditional publishers were first developing pay-to-publish divisions, I had a client that hired me to write his book and then manage the publishing process. The publisher used a designer that did a terrible job. I really had to fight to get the design changed to something that was decent. But I understood the process and I knew what to do. An author with no publishing experience probably wouldn't.

MM: Exactly.

JL: Years ago there were companies we called vanity presses that were little more than glorified printers. They'd produce a book, send you your several thousand copies, and that was it. How have those companies changed?

MM: I think those companies are what we now call subsidy publishers. They still exist and they're pervasive in self-publishing. They advertise everywhere, the same places that legitimate hybrid companies do. Or companies that are author-assisted. You have to be really careful that you check out the company you're going to publish with.

Some of the big ones are AuthorHouse, Outskirts Press, Balboa Press, iUniverse, Xlibris, Trafford House Publishing—there are quite a few of them, and I'm not the only to say you should beware of them. It's just that authors often don't know the industry and they don't know how these companies operate. They'll promise you the moon and the stars and charge a lot for it, but they end up holding your book hostage with extremely limiting contracts, where they control everything from the pricing of your book to the distribution. They can choose to sell as many or as few copies as they want. And you have no control over that—even your copyright. And if you want gain back control of your book, you have to pay through the nose to get out of the contract.

It's just like anything: If their promises sound too good to be true, they probably are. A lot of these companies will have very high-pressure tactics. If somebody is really pressuring you to publish with them, or promising you that you're going to be a bestseller, or say if you don't decide this by today, we're going to pull this price—those people are not good news.

The whole thing is they really don't care about selling your book because they're making their money on the production side. So you end up with no sales. They just want to get a lot of money from you. They'll claim the reason you don't have any sales is because you're not marketing, or the book isn't getting marketed well enough, so they'll try to aggressively upsell you expensive add-on marketing packages.

A lot of these companies just do really shoddy work. They have shoddy covers, terrible editing and proofreading, anemic book descriptions, poor formatting, incorrect attachment of metadata. They just really don't care about your book. All they care about is extracting as much of your money from you as possible.

JL: Are there any good subsidy publishers?

MM: Not that I know of. At its core, a subsidy publisher is really an author-assisted publisher where you pay for them to help you publish your book, and they do all the production for you, the editing, the design. You can find other companies like that that will help you do that, and are fine, as long as you make sure they're doing a quality job. But the difference is that a subsidy publisher really does not have the author at heart. Their whole point is to get money from you, to just take it and not do anything.

And if you've signed away your copyright, you're stuck. That's why it's really important that you don't give your copyright to anyone else. It's important that you keep your own copyright. A lot of these companies are going to try to take your copyright because they want complete control over your book so that you have to pay them money to do anything else with it.

JL: Many traditional publishers have added divisions that are essentially subsidy publishers. What's going on in that arena?

MM: It's economics. Many traditional publishers have purchased or merged with subsidy companies. The biggest and most notorious is Penguin Random House, which now owns AuthorHouse, which is nothing more than a subsidy publisher. It's a win-win for both companies.

Traditional publishers have realized that having these imprints is a fantastic way to make additional revenue on books that they wouldn't take on through traditional means. And the subsidy publisher gets more customers because being connected with a traditional publishing company gives them legitimacy in unwary authors' eyes.

JL: *What's the difference between using a subsidy publisher that you pay and who does everything for you verses self-publishing, where you do it all yourself, hire various services and pay for all of that?*

MM: Other than potentially in terms of quality, because subsidy publishes often do shoddy work, the difference is that it will cost a lot more to use a subsidy publisher. They charge a lot for these services. Also there's the loss of control. With a subsidy publisher, you think you have control, but you don't.

JL: *So pure self-publishing is more work for you, but you have more control, you can control your costs, quality, everything about the process.*

MM: Right. You get to control the quality, you can control the design, you can control the title, pricing, distribution. You have a lot more control when you self-publish. And it does take you more time if you're doing it on your own. Of course, there are ways to alleviate that as well. You can hire a project manager such as myself to do all that for you if you lack the time. But even if you don't hire a project manager, it may take you more time to manage it yourself, but you'll end up with a much better product.

You have to know: Do you have that control? Are you paying too much money? Are you getting that quality?

JL: How can authors avoid getting ripped off by these companies?

MM: I recently read a really good blog by Helen Sedwick, who is an author and an attorney, that listed seven questions to ask before choosing a self-publishing company. She says these questions will help you identify which companies will give you the greatest control over the process and result. You should be able to answer the first six by looking at the companies' websites. The last question may take a little more research.

Here are the questions she recommends asking and her explanation for how to evaluate the answers:

1. What is the lowest retail price you may set for your book? Some companies control the retail price of your print book and set it unrealistically high. One company claims its high pricing is author-friendly because it increases potential royalties. Forget it. You may have a terrific book, perfectly edited, with a beautiful cover and interior, but if it is priced at $20 alongside bestsellers priced at $15, $12, or $8, no one will buy it. To market your book successfully, the price must be competitive. Stay away from any company that will price your book out of the market. You should control the retail price of your book. Period.

2. What is the author price for your book (the price you pay per copy)? You will be buying a lot of books and giving them away to reviewers, bloggers, friends and family, or reselling them at readings, conferences, and through your website. Use a company that will sell your books to you at a reasonable price. Companies that set high retail prices typically offer to give their authors a scrawny 30 percent discount. So if they price your book at $19.95, you will pay $13.96 per copy, plus another $2 to $3 for shipping and handling. That's ridiculous. Traditional publishers typically set the price of authors' copies at a discount off the retail price, but in that case, you haven't paid the publisher to produce your book.

For a subsidy or author-assisted publisher, the author price should be the actual printing costs plus a reasonable markup (15-20 percent) and not a discount from the retail price. Why pay more for your copies because the company sets the retail price at $20 instead of $10? The printing costs are the same. You will have already paid the company hundreds, if not thousands, of dollars for design, editorial, and marketing services.

A company that sets a high retail price for your book is *not* expecting to make money by selling it to the public. They are going to make money selling it to you at a high author price.

3. What royalties will you earn? You should be able to calculate your royalties online by using different trim sizes, pages and retail pricing. Be suspicious of any company that did not have a royalty calculator on its website. If the website states that pricing, royalties and such cannot be determined until your manuscript is reviewed or formatted (and typically after you have given them your credit card number and paid a nonrefundable amount), keep going somewhere else.

4. Is the agreement exclusive or non-exclusive? You should never give a company exclusive rights to your work. And no options on any other works, formats, movie rights, subsidiary rights, either. These companies are not traditional publishers that have invested capital in your book and want to protect that investment. They are service providers only and are not entitled to exclusive rights or options.

You might not be able to answer this question without looking at the company's contract. A reputable one will post its contract online. Avoid any company that will not release its contract until you sign up.

5. Is it easy to terminate the agreement? You should have the right to terminate the relationship, with no more than 30 days' notice delivered via email. None of this certified mail, return receipt nonsense. After termination, the company may have the right to sell off its existing inventory, but that's it. It should *not* have the right to continue to print and sell your book, even if the right is non-exclusive.

6. Will you get production-ready files upon termination? If you terminate, the company should give you the final production-ready files of your cover and interior at no or low cost. Not PDFs of your print-ready files, but the actual, functional production files in Adobe InDesign. If you move your book to a new printer without the production-ready files, you'll have to create new files at considerable cost. It is outrageous for company to hold onto these files after you've paid for the design, editing, and layout work. You own the product and should control it.

7. What is the reputation of the company? Go to websites like Predators & Editors, Absolute Write Water Cooler, and Writers Beware and search for information about the company. Reviews may be available at *The Independent Publishing Magazine* site.

Every company will have its share of unhappy customers,

so sort through the complaints to get a sense of which ones are legitimate. If you find multiple reports from unhappy customers, stay far away.

Note: To read the full text of Helen Sedwick's blog, go to https://www.thebookdesigner.com/2014/06/7-questions-to-ask-before-choosing-a-self-publishing-company/.

FINDING SELF-PUBLISHING RESOURCES

JL: *It's unlikely that the average individual, especially a first-time author, would have the skills to take a book through the entire process from concept to published. What sort of help are they likely to need and where do they start looking for it? Let's say they've decided that they want to avoid the subsidy publishers, they don't have an existing platform, they've only got a small email list or none at all, and a major publisher wouldn't take them on. What help are they going to need to get their first book out there?*

MM: To get your first book out there, you're going to need a variety of contractors to help you. You're going to need an editor, you're going to need a cover designer and an interior designer. That's not always the same person. It frequently is, but it doesn't have to be.

You're going to need a proofreader, an indexer, and I would suggest that you also get a copywriter—somebody who is experienced in writing back cover copy, which is the description of your book. I have a lot of clients who want to try and save money there, and they write it themselves and then I edit it, but I don't think that's a good idea. It takes a real professional to do this. Sometimes people think they don't need that because their book may not end up in a bookstore, but a lot of people do read that copy on Amazon, because you can look at the back cover on Amazon. A lot of times that's also the description that you end up using on Amazon. So the back cover copy is really important. Just like the cover is important because it makes that powerful first impression, a lot of people read that description and if it doesn't immediately grab them, they're going to move on. It takes a special talent to be able to describe your book in a way that will grab people.

You'll also probably need help with marketing. You can do it yourself, but you still need to have resources. Or you need a marketing person, a public relations person or a publicist, if you want to hire that out.

JL: Where do you find those resources? Or even a project manager who might be able to find them for you? Talk about what a book project manager can do for you and how that is different from a subsidy publisher.

MM: To answer your question about a project manager: They go under different titles, it might be under project manager, you can also look under book shepherds. But this is basically somebody that guides you through the self-publishing process. You can do it all on your own but a lot of people don't have the time, because it takes a lot of time to find these various people and to manage them, and if you're running a successful business or you're doing your book part-time and you work full-time, you may not have the time do everything yourself. Or your time may be better spent doing other things besides managing your book's production process. So having a book shepherd or project manager to help you, to guide you through the process, takes a lot of the detail work away and lets you focus on the big picture. They will tell you exactly what you need to be doing at each step, or they will actually do everything for you.

If you don't have the time or aren't confident that you can figure it all out yourself, you could pay a project manager or book shepherd to manage the whole process. They will find all of the contractors you need for you. They'll find you an editor, they'll find you a designer, indexer, and these will be people that you can trust, if you vetted the project manager and you know that they work with good quality people. The people that I work with, I've worked with for over 20 years, and I know that they do very good work, they're reliable and they have the author's interest at heart.

Then, generally, all you have to do is approve each step. You approve the editing, you approve the cover, you approve the interior design. So it takes a lot of the pressure off of you.

JL: What advice do you have for how an author can find a reputable project manager?

MM: There are a lot of charlatans out there taking advantage of neophytes. Too often they look for the cheapest, fastest route, and they use vendors who don't have proven track records. Many project managers don't really have the experience to shepherd a book to success. Many of them are people who wrote and self-published a book, learned a bit along the way, then decided they could tell everybody else how to create a book. So, as they say, buyer beware—make sure you've done your due diligence to ensure the shepherd has the experience to back up their claims.

Along with experience, rapport is also a factor. Interview a few and make sure you have a connection. Do you feel comfortable speaking with them? Do they talk above you, or do they take time to explain things? Ask them to explain about their service.

JL: *What sort of questions should you ask when you're interviewing project managers?*

MM: Ask each shepherd you interview the same series of questions so you can compare. Some basic questions you should ask are:

- How much do you charge, and when are payments due?
- What is included in your fee?
- What is your background?
- Can I see some samples of the work you've done in my genre?
- Can I speak with you on the phone, or will correspondence be mostly through email? If via phone, is there a consultation fee?
- Will I be working directly with the freelancers, or will everything go through you?
- What are the hours I can reach you?
- Will you give me a selection of editors and designers, or do I have to go with one of your choosing?

Of course, also ask for references and check them.

A good project manager will also ask you some initial questions to make sure you're ready for prime time before you sign on the dotted line. Be prepared to answer questions about:

- Genre?
- Book synopsis?
- Target audience?
- Word count?
- Time-frame or desired launch date?
- How do you intend to market and distribute your book?
- Why are you qualified to write the book?
- Who is your competition (other books, websites, blogs)?

JL: How much do project managers typically charge?

MM: There are a variety of fee structures:

- Tiered flat-rate service packages, which include a project management fee, while fees for each service are opaque.
- A percentage is tacked onto the total project cost to cover project management.
- Hourly.
- Each portion of the project, including project management, is charged as a flat fee, itemized, and transparent.

Typically, you do not have to pay the whole fee upfront. It's usually due in portions, like 50 percent in advance, with the balance due upon printing. Or you pay in thirds. Or you pay as each vendor completes their portion, like editing, then cover design, then proofreading, etc.

JL: Where do you find project managers?

MM: There are a lot of ways to find good project managers, even if you don't have a lot of connections in the publishing industry. They include:

- Referrals and word-of-mouth. If you know people who have published a book, ask if they used a project manager and if they were happy with the service.
- Social media platforms.
- LinkedIn. Join groups, like the Book Publishing Professionals or the Independent Book Publishers Association. Ask for referrals or trawl the Q&As and look at the profiles of the shepherds who are influencers or whose responses you like.
- Twitter. Follow project managers and see if you like them, or other book professionals and ask for referrals.
- Association membership lists. Join national and local editorial groups and look at their membership lists or go to the meetings. A few of the groups I recommend are Editorial Freelancers Association, San Diego Professional Editors Network (SD/PEN); your Independent Book Publishers Association (IBPA) local chapter; and MediaBistro. If you want to publish a book, you should join one anyway for the wealth of information you'll get.
- Writer's or publishing conferences or Book Publishing University, hosted by the IBPA every year.

JL: Just to clarify: If you use a project manager, you still have full control, unlike with the subsidy publishers or even a traditional or hybrid publisher where you don't really have the final decision.

MM: Right.

JL: *Earlier you mentioned finding an indexer. How important is indexing?*

MM: It depends on the book. I think most nonfiction books need an index. Again, a lot of self-publishers try to save money there by not including an index. It isn't the cheapest thing to do. But I think that it's just another service that adds value for your readers. A lot of nonfiction books have a lot different topics in them, and an index will help the readers so they can find information easily after they've read it. They don't have to try and find it again in the book.

JL: *I think if it's a reference style, how-to kind of book, then you need an index. If it's more of a rah-rah, motivational book, I would think that the index would be less important.*

MM: Right.

JL: *I also read somewhere that if you're looking to avoid doing an index, one way to compensate for that is to do a detailed table of contents. Rather than just your chapter titles, include all your subtitles and that kind of thing. So the table of contents almost works as an index.*

MM: You could that. It's not as detailed as a complete index. But a key point to this whole discussion is to help people decide which route they want to go. If you decide you want to go the self-publishing route and you want it to be successful, as we've said, you really have to make it professional. Part of being a professional book is having an index.

JL: *Let's talk about finding and working with good service providers. Sometimes a publishing-related service provider such as a ghostwriter, editor, designer, marketer, whatever, isn't trying* *to scam you, but they just aren't very good or they're not a good match for your project. How do you find the quality providers? How do you vet them, and then then if there's a problem, how do you deal with it? Anybody can put themselves out there and say, "I'm an editor, I'm a ghostwriter, I design book covers." How do you know who are the good ones?*

MM: Something else you have to be careful about is that there are people who have published one book and decide they can hang out their shingle as a book publishing consultant. They think now they have this great system that they can tell other people how to do it. And now all of a sudden they're a book shepherd. But just because you've published one book does not make you qualified to do that for others.

Where you find good people is in other reputable situations. You can either find them from a referral, from somebody else who has worked with them. And that's a great way. Or you can go to LinkedIn, there are a lot of great publisher communities there, like the book publishers forum. You can troll around in there, ask questions and see what people recommend, and then investigate them. There are a lot of professional associations that offer referrals to their members. For example, the Editorial Freelancers Association is a great place to find a qualified editor. The Independent Book Publishers Association has a supplier and services database on their website. That's the two primary ways to find publishing service providers, either a referral or going through a professional organization.

JL: How would you answer this: I'm hiring a ghostwriter, a top-notch ghostwriter and I'm paying a lot of money for this person. Why do I need an editor?

MM: Even the best writers need editors. You need somebody objective to look at the manuscript. When you have a book edited, it goes through various stages. A lot of times it will go through an editor who might be a developmental editor, which means they're looking at the whole picture, and they might be changing the organization around, they might be rewriting paragraphs. Then it goes through a copy editor who just does line editing. Then a proofreader, who is looking at the very small details, looking for grammar and punctuation errors.

Each time it goes through one of these stages, somebody else is looking for something different, and you can't come up with a really great quality book if you just have one person looking at it or if the writer tries to edit it himself. Because there are things that are going to be missed. And in many cases, big things that will reflect poorly on you.

JL: Let's talk about audiobooks. What do authors who want to have an audio version of their book need to know about finding production sources?

MM: I would just say be careful. I've been to seminars and workshops on audiobooks and they try to tell you that you have to hire award-winning people to produce your book. It sounds like it is a really pricey proposition because they make you think that you have to hire these really pricey people, but you do *not* have to do that.

On the other hand, a lot of people think that they can do it themselves and I would caution people not to do that, because it's very difficult to produce a professional-sounding book. You can either go through ACX and have them produce it for them and you can independently hire the voice talent and an audiobook producer to do it for you. I have somebody that I work with who is wonderful and doesn't cost a lot of money.

JL: *If you have a problem with one of your service providers, how do you deal with it?*

MM: If you run into a problem with a subsidy publisher, you're in a pickle. A lot of times, you have to go a lawyer to take care of that. If you're just working with a designer, then you need to make sure that you have a contract that addresses what happens if there's a dispute. You can try talking to the person and see if they will be reasonable on their own, if they've done something that you don't agree with. And hopefully you'll be able to resolve it by just talking. Of course you want to do that first, but if you can't resolve it that way, you may have to escalate to legal action. That's why you need to make sure that you have a contract in place that will protect you.

JL: *I've had clients who didn't want to bother with the contract. They thought it was good enough to just accept my proposal, which basically just covers the price and scope of work, but not the details. This was an issue I discussed with Suzanne Meehle, who is the attorney I spoke with for the Conversations book,* Is Your Website Legal? How To Be Sure Your Website Won't Get You Sued, Shut Down or in Other Trouble. *We talked about how important it was to have a contract that addresses issues such who owns intellectual property like your website design and copy, and how you will resolve disputes. The same principles apply to dealing with service providers who help you self-publish your book.*

MM: Never let anybody talk you into not having a contract. You just never know. People seem really friendly and you think that nothing will ever happen because they seem like a good guy, or whatever. But you just never know. It's just always better to have that protection.

I've been fortunate that there's only been one time when I had to remind a supplier of the contract. The author wasn't happy with one of my vendors and I had to pull out the contract and remind her that she'd signed it. It was fortunate for me that I had the contract and was able to do that.

JL: Any advice for new authors in the area of promotion that we haven't already talked about?

MM: Like I said, you can either do it yourself or you can go and have a marketing firm or a publicist do it for you. Having somebody else do it could be very expensive. Most publicists will charge you in the range of $3,000-$6,000 for six months. And there's no guarantee that you're going to get your investment out of it. Shop around. There are marketing firms and publicist companies that are set up specifically for self-publishers. And you can get a deal with them—you can purchase things ala cart or you can maybe only pay for three months. Also you can get into a situation where you pay by the promotion. Say you just want somebody to promote a certain campaign for you. It's an ala cart thing. And there are different companies that do that.

In terms of doing it yourself, there are plenty of opportunities and places you can get information to do it yourself. One great source is John Kremer; he's the guru of do-it-yourself book marketing. His website is www.bookmarket. com. He wrote a book called *1001 Ways to Market Your Book.*

Another thing I suggest you join the Independent Book Publishers Association, because they have a lot of webinars that are really inexpensive. If you're a member, they're just $19 each. And you'll get great information. There's a woman named Amy Collins who keeps up with the best ways to sell your books on Amazon. I just listened to one of her webinars the other day through IBPA, and it had really, really valuable information. If you went to hear her speak, you would pay hundreds of dollars. Through the IBPA, too, you get all kinds of discounts. You not only get the education, you get all kinds of discounts on ISBNs, printers and all types of other vendors. It's really helpful. They have a two-day conference you can attend every year, you'll get scads of information. They also have chapters all over the country.

The more you talk to people, the more different ways you'll find to promote your book.

COST OF SELF-PUBLISHING

JL: We've talked about the fact that it costs money to produce a quality self-published book. What can an author expect to spend on things like cover design, interior design, editing?

MM: It varies so much. You could go to Fiverr or 99designs and get a cover for $99.

JL: And it will look like a cover that you bought for $99.

MM: For a competitive cover from a quality designer, you can spend anywhere from $600 on the low end to $3,500 if you want a designer who is award-winning. A middle ground probably about $1,500 for a competitive cover. I work with people of all budgets, and you can get a good cover for $600-$950.

The thing you have to be careful of is that the more artwork you add to the cover, the more expensive it is. The more complex the cover is, if you want a specific photo or you need an original illustration, all those things make the cover cost more. The same with the interior.

JL: What are the ranges for interior design?

MM: Interior design can range from about $5 up to $17 per page. A lot of people, if you work with them, will give you a flat rate for the book. Probably a middle ground would be around $8 a page.

Be careful and make sure you know what you're asking for. Some designers add on for different things. Some also charge not just per page, which they call a composition rate, for page composition, which means just flowing in the text and designing each page, they also charge a design fee at the outset. Which means they're charging you a separate fee to come up with that initial design and then to put your manuscript into the design.

Then cost of editing can vary. The most important thing with editing is make sure that you're getting the type of editing that you need. Because a lot of people aren't familiar with what each level of editing involves, they think they just need proofreading but they actually need more than that. Find an editor who will give you a free sample edit. I offer a free sample edit of five pages. That lets my clients see what kind of work I do and it helps me determine what level of editing that you need so I can create a proposal and price for you.

If you're talking about developmental editing, which is the highest level of editing, which is when you're looking at the book as a whole and doing everything from organizing to rewriting entire paragraphs, the cost of that is a lot higher than it is for if somebody is already a really good writer, like you are, Jackie, and who just needs copyediting or line editing. With copyediting or line editing, they're not reorganizing your book. They don't need to help you write transitions. They're just correcting grammar and punctuation, making sure the style is consistent and maybe they're rewriting awkward sentences.

Then there's proofreading, which is looking for formatting mistakes, or correcting grammar, punctuation and spelling mistakes.

The cost of all those things can really vary. Developmental editing can run anywhere from $50 to $100 an hour. Of course, you need to ask anyone you're considering working with how many hours they estimate they're going to spend on your project if they quote you an hourly rate.

A good place to go to get competitive rate information so you have a basis to start from in your negotiations, and so you know whether someone is too far off the mark, is go to the Editorial Freelancers Association. They have a page that has rates on it. And it will cover everything including copyediting, proofreading, research, ghostwriting, web editing, manuscript evaluation—it covers the gamut and it will give you the low and the high end of what people are charging. So at least you know whether someone you're considering is in the ballpark of the going rates in the market.

JL: *Taking a look at that can help you plan your initial budget, too. I've asked people what their budget is and they have no idea because they don't know what the costs are.*

MM: Right. Do a little research before you start contacting people so you have some type of budget in mind, so that you're not wasting your time or the time of the contractor that you're speaking to. I've gotten calls from people who didn't want to share their budget upfront. But if you only have $1,000 to work with, you're not going to get an 80,000-word book edited for that.

JL: *I think a lot of times the reason people don't want to tell you their budget is that they think you'll automatically come in with a fee that will take up the entire budget. But legitimate professional service providers don't ask what your budget is because they want to charge you more or come in at the high end of what you're willing to spend. They need to know if you've got a realistic picture of what you'll need to spend to get the whole project done. Also it helps guide them in saying, "If you're budget is only this much, this is how much I can do for you."*

MM: Which brings up a point I think is important. If a contractor you're interested in working with comes back with price that's too high, talk to that person before you go to someone else. I've had people go to someone else because they thought the price I quoted was too high. But going with the low price is not always the smartest decision. The cheaper service may not be as good and you won't get the quality you want.

If you want to work with a particular provider but you can't afford the fee they quoted, be honest. Talk to them. You might able to work something out. Maybe you can have them work up to a certain number of hours and see where you are. Or maybe the person will work on installments, getting paid as the project moves along. Or maybe the person can reduce some of the work to lower the cost. The point is, talk to them. Ask what they can do. Remember that the cheapest person isn't necessarily the best person for the job, and your book is a reflection of you.

I've had clients who came to me because they went with the cheapest person and that person didn't do a good job, and now the client is coming to me to fix it. And they're going to end up spending more than they would have if they had just gone to somebody who was a professional who did quality work in the first place.

As with any purchase, it's buyer beware. Do your homework. Be sure you know what you're getting for what you're paying.

JL: *Before we wrap up, do you have any final thoughts?*

MM: Which way you decide to go—self-publishing, traditional publishing or one of the hybrid variations—depends on what your goals are, how much time you have, how much money you want to spend, and how much control you want.

If you're the type of person who is absolutely insistent and your dream is to be published by a traditional publisher, and you're willing to wait the time it takes, go for it. I worked with a lawyer one time, he was a lawyer with a big law firm, and he had all the money in the world to be able to self-publish, he could have sold lots of books on his own, and I told him that. But he really wanted to have that panache of having a traditional publisher's imprint on the spine of his book. That was really important to him.

If you don't want to wait and you want the most control over your book, and you have the money to invest in quality publishing and getting a quality editor, designer, and so forth—because those services aren't cheap—then self-publishing is the way you want to go. Because you get to control everything from the title to the content to who you're going to market it to, and you also get all of the profits.

If you decide to take the self-publishing route, I encourage you to join the Independent Book Publishers Association (IBPA). It's a great organization, it doesn't cost a lot, and you'll get valuable information and contacts.

JL: Just in the last few years, we've seen huge changes in the independent publishing industry. What are your predictions for the future?

MM: I think it is going to continue to go in the direction that it is—it's going to grow and become more professional. More and more authors will turn to independent publishing and the lines between indie and traditional publishing will be more and more blurred. There are going to be more avenues, more choices for authors to get their books published and there's going to be less to distinguish between indie published and traditionally published books.

~~~

Learn more about and connect with Marla Markman at MarlaMarkman.com

APPENDIX 2

How to Avoid Being Ripped Off by a Publisher

Ask These Important Questions Before You Pay to Publish Your Book

Jacquelyn Lynn

INTRODUCTION

HOW MUCH SHOULD YOU expect to pay to have your book published?

Like just about everything else in our world, changes in the publishing industry are happening quickly, and it's hard to keep up.

Today's publishing world is dominated by three primary business models:

Traditional publishing, where publishers contract with authors and pay royalties on book sales.

Self-publishing, where authors do all the publishing work themselves.

Hybrid or pay-to-publish, where a company does the work traditional publishers do but authors pay the costs.

We've seen a tremendous proliferation of hybrid and pay-to-publish companies. These companies operate similarly to traditional publishers except the have the financial protection of the author paying all the costs of publishing their book. Paying to get your book published no longer carries the stigma it once did, but it still carries risk.

Pay-to-publish companies are sometimes referred

to as *hybrid publishers* or *vanity presses*. I use the term pay-to-publish because it clearly describes how these companies function. They may be independent operations or subsidiaries of traditional publishers.

Some pay-to-publish companies are legitimate options for authors who are either unable to or choose not to go with a traditional publishing house; others are, to put it simply, rip-offs.

The scam pay-to-publish operations play on the emotions of aspiring authors, making unrealistic promises, charging exorbitant fees that the authors will never recover, and often producing poor quality books.

So how can you tell the difference? Conduct thorough due diligence. Ask these questions before you sign a contract and pay any money.

ABOUT THE PUBLISHER

Don't get so excited about having your book published that you forget the fundamental fact that in a pay-to-publish relationship, you are the customer, and the publisher is providing a service. Just as you would research any company from which you make a major purchase, research the publisher.

How long have you been in been in business?

Many hybrid publishers are relatively young companies. That in itself is not a reason to reject the company, but it's something you should know.

Is the company independent or owned by a parent corporation?

Many traditional publishers have established pay-to-publish subsidiaries. If another corporation owns the company you're considering, you'll want to research that entity as well.

What are the company's imprints?

A publisher's imprint is the trade name under which it publishes its books. It's common for publishers to have multiple imprints that they use as brands to market works to various consumer segments.

What imprint will be shown as the publisher of my book?

Research that imprint and be sure it has a reputation you want to be associated with, both in how it does business and what other titles it publishes.

Who are the company's principals? What are their backgrounds?

The founder(s), officers, and key executives should be listed on the publisher's website, but if they're not, ask. In addition to reading what the company has to say about the principals, research them independently. Check out their social media pages. Do a general internet search to see what's been said and written about them and what they may have published.

What are the genres of the books you publish? How many books a year do you publish?

The two different types of books are fiction (a story the author made up) and nonfiction (factual information). Under those two types are dozens of categories, or genres, which are characterized by similarities in form, style, or subject matter.

It's best if the publisher you choose is experienced in your book's genre and has an appropriate team of editors, designers, proofreaders, and so on. For example, if you've written a romantic suspense novel and 90 percent of the publisher's titles are nonfiction how-to and business books, the company may not be the best fit for you.

Find out how many books a year they publish to determine the size and scope of their operation. As a follow-up, ask how many books they publish in your specific genre each year.

Who will I be working with?

What team members will you be interacting with, and who will your primary contact be? It's likely that this will not be the person you initially worked with. In most pay-to-publish operations, the individual who handles acquisitions is primarily a salesperson. Once you sign the contract, you'll likely be handed off to a project manager who will coordinate all the elements of the publishing process. There's nothing wrong with this; in fact, it's an efficient use of skills. But you should know ahead of time, and you may even want to meet (either in person or virtually) with the project manager before you make a commitment.

You may also want to find out if the team members you'll be dealing with work virtually or onsite. That shouldn't affect the quality of their work, but it could impact how the work flows and how you communicate. Related to that is asking if they're independent contractors or employees. While the status of their employment relationship with the publisher isn't likely to affect their work, knowing that gives you an idea of how the company operates.

How will communications be handled?

Will you be communicating primarily through email? Within documents stored in the cloud? On the publisher's dashboard? By phone?

The publisher likely has a standard system in place for all its authors. Be sure you understand and are comfortable with the publisher's communication methods.

After every telephone or online conversation, follow up with an email confirming your understanding of what was said and agreed to.

May I see the contract before we finalize it?

Ask to see the publisher's standard contract early in the negotiation (sales) process. All publishing agreements begin with a template. Seeing that template before it's finalized with the details of your project will give you a better understanding of how the publisher functions.

Be sure you understand every word of the contract and ask questions about anything that doesn't make sense to you. Remember that the contract will be written to the publisher's advantage (that's what their lawyers are paid to do); don't be afraid to ask for changes that benefit you.

When your negotiations have advanced to the point that you're ready to finalize the contract with your book's information, have a lawyer experienced in intellectual property and publishing review it. Yes, it may cost you a few hundred dollars, but you're considering an investment of thousands. If you don't spend the money on an attorney who understands the business, don't get upset if you get ripped off.

Don't let a publisher dismiss your concerns about contract language by saying something is standard or never enforced. Whatever it is, if it's in the contract, it's enforceable. If it's not necessary, take it out.

Every promise the publisher makes should be in the contract. If it's not, it's not enforceable.

Insisting on a clear, complete, understandable contract does not indicate a lack of trust. Rather, it indicates a desire for accurate communication.

PUBLISHING DETAILS

Some of these questions may have been answered in the standard contract. If they weren't, ask them before you finalize your agreement.

Who holds the copyright?

A copyright is valuable intellectual property. Typically, the copyright is held by the named author of the work, but the copyright issue goes beyond that. For a publisher (either traditional or pay-to-publish) to produce your book, you must assign the necessary rights to it. That's standard in the industry.

What you need to understand is exactly what rights you're assigning to the publisher, along with when and under what circumstances that assignment ends. Those rights could include various formats (print, electronic, video, audio, and more); translations into other languages; and derivative works (film, television shows, plays, condensations, and more). Some copyright issues are governed by the Copyright Act; others by your agreement. For example, your agreement should indicate what happens if the publisher files bankruptcy, goes out of business, or is sold.

Ask about the copyright and be sure you understand the full scope of the assignment you're making.

In what formats will my book be published?

Will your book be published in hardcover, softcover (paperback), and ebook formats? What about an audio version? The initial answer to this question will drive further discussion and negotiation.

Who sets the retail price of the book?

Many considerations go into setting the book's retail price, including the cost of production, the genre, the market, and more. If your book is priced too high, it won't sell. As important as that is to you, it's not a big deal to a pay-to-publish company because they made their profit from you and book sales aren't important to them.

Too many authors have trusted their pay-to-publish company on this issue and ended up with an overpriced book that no one will buy.

What happens if the contracted schedule isn't met?

Your agreement should include a publication date and schedule of work deadlines, such as when your manuscript is due, how long it will take for editing, how much time you have to approve or reject the editor's changes, how long the cover and interior design process will take, and so on. Ask what happens if that schedule isn't met on either side.

For example, what if the assigned editor has a personal situation and doesn't get your manuscript back to you on schedule? What if you need more time to review the editor's input? These are routine occurrences in the publishing industry. Of course, it's expected that everyone will work together to address any issues reasonably, but you want a sense of how the unexpected will be handled ahead of time.

What is your cancellation/termination policy?

What happens to your agreement if you don't complete the book or you want to cancel the contract before the book is published?

ROYALTIES AND COST OF SERVICES

In traditional publishing, money typically flows one way: from the publisher to the author (except when the author is buying copies of their book) in the form of advances and royalties. In a pay-to-publish situation, the money flows two ways: from the author to the publisher for various publishing-related services and from the publisher to the author in the form of royalties. Royalties are the portion of the sale that the publisher pays you when someone buys your book. Ask these questions:

What is the total cost?

Find out the total amount you'll have to pay to get your book published. You might hear things like, "We can get started for" a relatively low amount. That's fine, but what's the bottom line?

Related to this is to ask if there will be any additional charges as you go along. Pay-to-publish operations have been known to get your book in production then suggest add-on packages such as marketing, promotion, distribution, and so on. The pressure to purchase these extras is intense.

Also ask about the payment schedule. You'll typically make payments in increments as the work progresses. Get that schedule so you can plan your budget.

How are royalties calculated and paid?

Royalty rates from traditional publishers are typically 5 to 15 percent of the retail sales price—or anywhere from .75 to $2.25 per copy for a book that sells for $15. This makes sense because a traditional publisher has covered all the costs of producing the book. Under a pay-to-publish agreement, you have paid all of the costs and should get a much larger percentage of each sale.

Ask when and how (check, electronic transfer) royalty payments are made. It's common for traditional publishers to pay royalties twice a year. But Amazon pays its publishers monthly. You'll also want to know if there's a minimum threshold for payments; that is, if your royalties are less than a certain amount, will the publisher hold those funds until your sales reach a stated amount?

How many books can I expect to sell?

No publisher can guarantee book sales. Traditional publishers look to their own market experience and research done by authors to estimate book sales. A legitimate pay-to-publish company will encourage you to do your own research to determine potential sales. Optimistic estimates or using other authors' performance to predict your sales is a sign that you may be talking with a less-than-reputable company.

AUTHOR COPIES

One of the most exciting times in the publishing process is when you hold the first copy of your book in your hands. But there are questions about author copies you should ask.

How many copies do I have to buy?

Some pay-to-publish companies don't charge for their services but require you to buy thousands of copies of your book. For example, if you buy 3,000 copies at $12 per copy, that's $36,000 plus tax, shipping, and storage (3,000 copies of any book take up a lot of space). Your book purchase has more than covered the publisher's costs of providing their services.

This might work for authors with an established audience. If you do public speaking and can sell books at the back of the room, or if you teach classes and include the book as part of what students get for their tuition, you may agree to these terms. But if you don't already have this system in place—that is, the speeches scheduled (where an average of 5-10 percent of the audience will buy a book), the email list built, the classes planned—approach this deal with caution. The reality is that most authors buy those 3,000 books, sell a few, give some away, and end up with 2,900 books in their garage.

Remember that the books you buy must be safely stored and then transported to wherever your buyers are. If you're selling books on your website, you'll have to package and ship each order. Be sure you have the facilities and equipment to accommodate that before agreeing to an arrangement like this.

Also, compare what you would pay if you paid for the cost of production services and bought books in smaller quantities.

How much do I have to pay for author copies? Are there any quantity discounts?

How much will you have to pay for the copies you buy? Is your author copy price based on the wholesale or retail price of the book? Is there a minimum amount you must order? Will larger orders earn a discount?

Also ask if you'll be charged sales tax on author copies. Specific sales tax rules vary by state, but in general, if you have a sales tax ID number or can get one, you shouldn't have to pay sales tax on copies you buy to resell.

Finally, ask how long it takes for your author copies to be produced and delivered.

EDITING AND PROOFREADING

Some pay-to-publish operations are little more than glorified printers—they'll take exactly what you give them and publish it. But even the best writers can benefit from editing, and every book needs to be proofed. Get clear answers to these questions:

What type of editing will be done on my book? What is the editing process?

What type of editing does the publisher offer? Editing is another one of those publishing terms with a range of definitions, so be sure you know what you're getting.

Developmental or conceptual editing usually happens early in the process, usually before the book is written. This is a big-picture look at your book to make sure that it's well-structured and complete.

Content or substantive editing includes a look at your book's structure but focuses on the construction of your manuscript, making sure it flows well, that stories and ideas are complete, and that the tone and voice are consistent.

A line edit is, as the name indicates, a line-by-line review of grammar, sentence construction, word usage, and how the sentences flow.

When your book is finished and the content and line editing are complete, it's time for a copyedit. This is the process of going through your book word by word, checking for spelling, punctuation, and grammar errors, and making sure your book conforms to the appropriate style guide.

Ask the publisher to describe the type of editing and the process that will be used. Will you be able to work directly with the editor to discuss issues? How will the editor present the changes to you (electronically or on paper)? What happens if you disagree with the editor?

What style guide does the publisher use?

A style guide is a set of standards for writing, formatting, and designing documents. Following a style guide provides a consistent experience for your reader.

The most widely used style guide in book publishing is the *Chicago Manual of Style* (CMOS).

Will the editor set up a style sheet for my book?

There may be circumstances when an author needs a style sheet that covers details not in CMOS. A business or technical book may use terms that need to be consistent. A fantasy novel set in a fictitious place or with characters that speak a language the author made up will need special attention to ensure all the invented words and locations are consistently used. Ask if the editor will create a style sheet or if you can create one for the editor to use.

What is the proofreading process?

Ideally, your book should have a minimum of two professional proofreads. One should be after your manuscript is edited and you have accepted or rejected the edits, and another after the book is produced and printed before it's published. Your manuscript may be absolutely perfect but glitches may show up when it's moved into the design software. It's not enough for the publisher to say your book will be proofed; ask for the process to be described in detail.

Will I get a proof copy of the book before it's released?

You should get at least one physical copy of the book to proof before it's officially published. Many publishers offer electronic proofs. While these are useful, nothing beats having a copy of your book in your hands for proofing.

You may also ask for extra proof copies to use as advance reader copies as part of your marketing efforts.

How are errors and updates handled after the book is published?

No matter how careful you are with editing and proofreading, there's always a chance an error will slip through or information will need to be updated. Find out the cost and procedure for minor corrections should they be necessary.

Will you register my book with the US Copyright Office?

Your book does not require formal registration to be protected under US copyright law, and many self-published authors don't bother with this step. However, there are some benefits to registration, and publishers typically handle this for their authors. The US Copyright Office charges a registration fee. Find out if the pay-to-publish company will handle this step and how much they charge, then decide if you want to handle it yourself. It's not difficult.

Will you secure a Library of Congress Control Number (LCCN) and create the Catalog in Publication (CIP) data?

This is especially important if you want your book in libraries or bookstores.

A Library of Congress catalog control number is a unique identification number that the Library of Congress assigns to the catalog record created for each book in its cataloged collections. Librarians use it to locate a specific Library of Congress catalog record in the national databases and to order catalog cards from the Library of Congress or from commercial suppliers. ... "CIP data" is the bibliographic record that appears printed on the verso of the book's title page. (Source: Library of Congress)

It's a simple process, and there are no registration fees. An experienced publisher will have a system in place to do this automatically.

In two minutes or 250 words (depending on whether you're talking or emailing), what exactly will you do for me and my book?

This will tell you how well the person you're dealing with understands the company and the industry.

INTERIOR AND COVER DESIGN

There's a lot more involved in producing a quality book than writing and editing. This is often a primary reason why authors choose a pay-to-publish company over self-publishing. You should know the answers to these questions before you get started.

What is the design process?

Get an overview of the design process for both the cover and the interior. You should have the opportunity to provide input to both designers before they begin and as the work progresses. Find out the procedure for making changes and how many revisions you can make.

How many cover design choices will I be given, and what happens if I don't like any of them?

Sometimes the cover designer's first effort will be exactly what you want; other times, it may take several versions to find the right one. Though you may hear stories of a designer doing 20, 30, or more designs before the author is happy, that will only happen when the designer, author, and publisher are not communicating effectively.

Who owns the cover design?

Under US copyright law, the artist who creates the book cover owns the copyright unless and until it is transferred to you or another entity. Be sure this is clearly stated in your agreement. Unless otherwise stipulated, the artist retains ownership of the designs you reject.

If the publisher or designers provide any images for the cover or interior, where are they from, and who owns the rights to them?

It's common for cover designers to use stock photography in their work. Be sure they have purchased the appropriate rights to use the image(s) and that those rights will transfer to you. If the publisher's services include creating interior graphics, your contract should clearly state who owns that work—and it should be you.

Related to the issue of using stock photos: Most

stock images are available to anyone who subscribes to the image service, which means you may see the same image on or in different books. You may want to insist that your cover and any other graphics be originally designed for your book without any elements from other sources.

PRINTING

How and where your book is printed will impact the quality of your book and the speed with which you'll receive your copies. Ask these questions:

What printing process will be used—offset or digital?

Offset printing is a commercial printing process in which an inked image is transferred from a plate to a rubber cylinder to paper or other material. Digital printing prints a digital-based image directly to a variety of media without a printing plate. Digital printing is the technology behind print-on-demand (POD) publishing, which allows books to be quickly printed after they are ordered.

As a general rule, offset printing is used for larger print runs (typically 500 or more copies of a book) and digital for smaller ones.

Where will my book be printed?

Overseas offset printers can produce quality books, especially in large quantities. The location of the printer and available transport will impact how long it will take your copies to be delivered.

For some authors, the printer's location may be a political or social issue. If this is important to you, be sure it's addressed in your contract.

What are the print run details?

Find out how many copies will be printed in the first run and where those books will be stored.

MARKETING

One of the biggest challenges for most authors is marketing their books. Many pay-to-publish companies offer marketing support in their packages. You'll need to do some research to determine the value of what they offer. Questions to ask include:

Do you offer marketing services?

If they offer marketing support, what's included in your basic contract, and what do you pay extra for? Exactly what will they do for you, and what do they expect you to do yourself? Who is your contact person, and how does the process work?

Will you create the marketing copy for my book?

Basic book marketing copy includes the back cover copy for your book, the book description (for online booksellers and your website), author bio, press release(s), and other elements in your media kit.

Do you coordinate marketing efforts among your authors to cross-promote their books?

This is not common, but it's worth asking about, especially to get early reviews on your book.

OTHER SERVICES

Because every pay-to-publish company is different, it's a good idea to find out if there are any available services you haven't discussed yet.

Do you offer coaching?

If so, find out precisely what's involved and how it's delivered. How is the process measured? Will you have a one-to-one relationship with your coach? What are the coach's credentials and qualifications?

What other services do you offer?

You never know what kind of a response you'll get to this question. Have fun with it.

DISTRIBUTION

Amazon has a huge share of the book market, but there are still plenty of other avenues for book distribution you should explore.

How will my book be distributed?

Expect that your book will be available on Amazon, but where else? Will it be available to bookstores? Libraries? Non-bookstore retailers such as gift shops and specialty stores?

What will you do to help get my book into retail stores?

For retail stores to consider your book, it must be priced right with an appropriate wholesale discount. It must include specific design elements, such as the category/genre and a retail barcode on the back cover and Library of Congress data on the copyright page. It must be available through the distributors bookstores use.

What online platforms besides Amazon will carry my book?

Your physical book should be available on Barnes & Noble, Walmart, and other major online booksellers. Whether you want the ebook version to be available only on Amazon or on other platforms (Apple, Kobo, etc.) is a decision you need to make based on your marketing strategy.

BEYOND THESE QUESTIONS

If you're satisfied with the answers you've gotten to these questions, ask to see some of the books they've published and read them. Look for typos, errors, poor editing, substandard design. Compare them to books published by major traditional publishers.

Talk to their other clients/authors. Ask them:

1. How responsive is the publisher?
2. How happy were they with the publisher?
3. How did their book do (sales, etc.)?
4. Would they publish with this company again?

Watch for typical red flags, such as being pressured to move quickly or assurances of a strong return on your investment. Do an online search of the company and its key personnel to see what others think of them.

RESOURCES

SELF-PUBLISHERS NEED A LOT of resources. Rather than include a list in this book that would be out of date within a few weeks of publication, I have set up a Resources page on my website.

An up-to-date list of the resources I use and recommend can be found at:

CreateTeachInspire.com/resources

GLOSSARY

Advance: In publishing, money paid to an author before a book is published. The advance is paid against future royalties, which means the author does not receive additional payments until the book has earned more in royalties than the amount of the advance.

Backlist: A publisher's list of older titles that are still in print, as distinguished from titles that are newly published.

Beta readers: Unpaid test readers who provide the author with feedback from the perspective of an average reader.

BISAC: Acronym for Book Industry Standards and Communication. The BISAC Subject Heading list is an industry-approved list of subject descriptors, each of which is represented by a nine-character alphanumeric code. Visit bisg.org for more information.

Book Industry Standards and Communication: See BISAC.

Callout: In book design, a short string of text (a sentence or two lifted from the main text or from some other source) set aside as a design element to provide visual interest to the page.

Copyediting: A type of editing that generally checks the work for accuracy and consistency in punctuation, spelling, grammatical structure, style, etc. Light copyediting is also known as baseline editing (spelling, grammar, punctuation, usage). Medium to heavy copyediting includes baseline editing plus changing texts and headings where appropriate; flagging ambiguous or incorrect statements; checking previews, summaries and end-of-chapter questions for accurate reflection of content; eliminating wordiness and inappropriate jargon, smoothing transitions, moving sentences to improve readability, and sometimes even rewriting.

Copyright: A form of protection provided by the laws of the United States for "original works of authorship," including literary, dramatic, musical, architectural, cartographic, choreographic, pantomimic, pictorial, graphic, sculptural, and audiovisual creations. "Copyright" literally means the right to copy but has come to mean that body of exclusive rights granted by law to copyright owners for protection of their work. Copyright protection does not extend to any idea, procedure, process, system, title, principle, or discovery. Similarly, names, titles, short phrases, slogans, familiar symbols, mere variations of typographic ornamentation, lettering, coloring, and listings of contents or ingredients are not subject to copyright.

Copyright notice: The copyright notice consists of three elements. They are the "c" in a circle (©), the year of first publication, and the name of the owner of copyright. A copyright notice is no longer legally required to secure copyright on works first published on or after March 1, 1989, but it does provide legal benefits.

Copyright page: A page in a book which lists publication, legal, copyright, printing, listing, and ISBN information.

Cover copy: The text on the cover of the book. The front cover copy is typically the title, subtitles, and author's name and may include a testimonial or other brief text. The back cover copy can include a description of the book and/or endorsements, and is designed to sell the book.

Developmental editing: A type of editing done before or during the production of a manuscript, generally in the area of nonfiction writing, to help the author develop ideas into a coherent, readable work. The developmental editor may help plan the book's organization, features and other aspects of the project.

Drop cap: A drop cap (dropped capital) is a large capital letter used as a decorative element at the beginning of a paragraph or section that drops two or more lines below the first line of the paragraph.

Ebook: An electronic version of a book that can be read on a computer or handheld device (e-reader) designed for that purpose.

Ghostwriter: A person who writes material (articles, books, blogs, etc.) for someone else who is the named author. The ghostwriter may or may not receive credit in the publication.

Half title page: A page containing nothing but the title of the book, often the first page in a printed book.

Hybrid publisher: A publishing model in which the publisher offers many of the same services that traditional publishers do but charge the authors. Also known as pay-to-publish and sometimes as partnership publishing.

IBPA: See Independent Book Publishers Association.

Independent (indie) publisher: A self-publisher, author-publisher, do-it-yourself publisher or traditional publisher not affiliated with any large corporation or conglomerate.

Independent Book Publishers Association (IBPA): a not-for-profit membership organization serving and leading the independent publishing community through advocacy, education, and tools for success. Visit ibpa-online.org for more information.

Independent publishing: See self-publishing.

International Standard Book Number: See ISBN.

ISBN: Acronym for International Standard Book Number. A 13-digit number assigned by standard book numbering agencies to control and facilitate activities within the publishing industry.

Line editing: A type of editing that addresses the quality of the prose, removes unnecessary repetition, restructures sentences and paragraphs to improve the flow, checks word usage, checks for style, consistency, flow and tone.

Literary agent: A professional agent who acts on behalf of an author in dealing with publishers and others involved in promoting the author's work.

Negative space: See white space.

Partnership publishing: See hybrid publisher.

Pay-to-publish: See hybrid publisher.

POD: See print-on-demand.

Print-on-demand: A printing technology and business process in which copies of a book or other document are not printed until an order has been received. This allows books to printed one at a time or in small quantities. Also referred to as POD.

Proofreading: The process of reviewing the final draft of a document to ensure consistency and accuracy in grammar, spelling, punctuation, and formatting.

Royalties: In publishing, the amount a publisher agrees to pay an author for the right to publish their book. Royalties are typically expressed as a percentage of sales.

Running head: In book design, a page header that appears at the top of each standard page. On facing pages, the head on one side may be different from the head on the other; for example, the author's name may be on the left page and the book's title on the right. Running heads are typically not included on blank pages, the first page of each chapter, and on other non-standard page.

Self-publishing: A publishing model in which

authors publish their books themselves by handling all of the work or hiring subcontractors such as editors or cover designs to provide specific functions. Some self-publishers hire a project manager to coordinate the process. Also known as independent or indie publishing.

Sensitivity readers: Readers who review manuscripts for issues of representation, bias, insensitive language, and cultural inaccuracies.

Sidebar: A short article set aside in a box or by using another graphic element that contains additional or explanatory material regarding the main subject.

Style guide: See style sheet.

Style sheet: A detailed list of the house style of a particular publisher, company, or publication. Style sheets provide a reference that assures consistency throughout a publication. Also known as a style guide.

Tagline: A short slogan used to reinforce a key aspect of a product or brand.

Title page: A page in a book which lists the full title, subtitle, author, publisher and edition.

Traditional publishing: A publishing model in which the publisher buys the rights to publish a book and pays the authors a percentage of the sales (royalties). Authors do not pay traditional publishers to publish their book and may receive an advance against royalties. Traditional publishers do all of the book's production work such as editing, cover design, interior design, and so on, as well as handle distribution and some marketing.

Trim size: The final size of a printed page or book.

US Copyright Office: The US government body that maintains records of copyright registration in the United States. Visit copyright.gov for more information.

US Patent and Trademark Office (PTO): The federal agency responsible for granting US patents and registering trademarks. Visit uspto.gov for more information.

White space: In page layout, the portion of the page left unmarked, including margins, gutters, space between lines and columns, graphics, or other objects. White space, also known as negative space, is an important design element. See also negative space.

ACKNOWLEDGEMENTS

As always, my first and most important acknowledgement goes to Jerry D. Clement, my husband and my partner in life and in business, who has been with me on this self-publishing journey from the beginning.

When I said, "We need to figure this out so we can offer this service to our clients," he said, "Let's do it!" When I said, "Let's produce a video series on self-publishing," he set up the cameras and lights. When I said, "Let's publish a book that will help people navigate the self-publishing process so they won't get ripped off," he said, "That's a great idea." When I said, "Let's do a second edition of *Simple Facts About Self-Publishing*," he said, "What do you need me to do?"

I'm also grateful to all the wonderful clients over the years whose projects have helped me grow professionally—especially the ones who said yes when I said, "I've never done that before, but I can figure it out."

Special thanks go to a mystery person on Facebook. In a conversation with a member of a writers/publishers group, I mentioned the first edition of this book. That person asked when it was published, and the question made me realize it was ready to be updated.

With eternal gratitude,
Jacquelyn Lynn

JACQUELYN LYNN is an inspirational author, business writer and ghostwriter, independent publisher, and publishing consultant. She is the author or ghostwriter of more than 45 books plus thousands of articles, blogs, ebooks, newsletters, white papers, and more.

She and her husband, Jerry D. Clement, are the managers of Tuscawilla Creative Services, LLC, a boutique publishing and consulting firm that God owns in Central Florida. As a team, they write and produce their own books and assist their clients through all aspects of creating and publishing books and other materials.

Learn more and connect with them at

CreateTeachInspire.com

Jacquelyn and Jerry would love to continue to support you with their Shareable Saturday messages. Receive a scripture and inspirational thought delivered to your inbox every Saturday morning. Sign up at **CreateTeachInspire.com/ss.**

www.ingramcontent.com/pod-product-compliance
Lightning Source LLC
Chambersburg PA
CBHW022050020426
42335CB00012B/624